CISI Certified Financial Planner of the Year

WARREN SHUTE

THE MONEY PLAN

Clear your debts, secure your tomorrow
and **live for today**

RETHINK PRESS

First published in Great Britain 2018
by Rethink Press (www.rethinkpress.com)

© Copyright Warren Shute

PRAISE

In *The Money Plan*, Warren Shute has laid out a step-by-step guide to achieving financial mastery. No matter what stage you are at in your personal finance journey, this book will help you take the next step, and then the one after that, until your financial future is secured. Read, digest and act – your future self will thank you for it.

Pete Matthew, Chartered Financial Planner, Founder of the MeaningfulMoney Podcast

This really is a must-read for anyone who is interested in their personal finances. Warren shares his 20+ years' experience in financial planning and has created a clear step-by-step process to help, from debt repayment to wealth building. I wish my clients had access to this years ago!

Aynsley Damery FCA, Tayabali Tomlin Accountants

A brilliant book which outlines a simple 5-step process to take you from where you are today to what we all want to achieve – financial independence in a book.

Carl Reader FCCA, CarlReader.com, author of Start-Up Coach and Franchising Handbook

The best thing you can do to master your money situation is to speak to Warren Shute. The second best thing is to read his book.

Michael Tipper, MichaelTipper.com

CONTENTS

Foreword by Alvin Hall

Introduction – Meeting Mr Planner   1

STAGE ONE – GOALS   **17**
Chapter 1 – What's Your Why?   19
• What are your Values?   21
• Follow your Values   23
• Summary   37

Chapter 2 – Goal setting   39
• 90 Day Check-Ins   44
• Summary   47

Chapter 3 – Set Yourself Up for Financial Success   49
• Summary   54

STAGE TWO – ORGANISED   **55**
Chapter 4 – Get Financially Well Organised Step One   57
• The Bank Account System   59
• Summary   72

Chapter 5 – Get Financially Well Organised Step Two   73
• Maximise Income   73
• Summary   80

Chapter 6 – Get Financially Well Organised Steps Three and Four   81
• Step One - Be Up to Date   83
• Step Two – Look at Interest Rates   84
• Step Three – Save £1000   85
• Summary   88

STAGE THREE – PROTECT   **89**

Chapter 7 – House Of Wealth Overview   91

- Financial Foundations   93
- Financial Security   112
- Financial Independence   113
- Financial Freedom   114
- Summary   115
- A summary of your foundation needs   116

STAGE FOUR – DEBT   **119**

Chapter 8 – Clearing The Debt Burden   121

- The Snowball   121
- Save your Emergency Fund   126
- Summary   129

Chapter 9 – 40/40/20   131

- Summary   138

Chapter 10 – Mortgage Snowball   139

- Summary   149

STAGE FIVE – INVEST   **151**

Chapter 11 – Investment Success   153

- Pensions First   157
- How Much to Save   160
- Workplace Pensions   163
- LISAs – Lifetime Individual Savings Accounts   165
- Pension Consolidation   165
- Defined Benefit Transfer   168
- Summary   169

Conclusion – Believing In Yourself   171

Final Thoughts   175

Appendix   179

Acknowledgements   181

Author Bio   184

Do you really want £1,000,000,
or what £1,000,000 can give you?

FOREWORD

In this book, Warren Shute shares with readers 20-plus years of what he has experienced and learned working face-to-face with clients in financial services. He has talked with them about their financial goals, their money worries, their retirement dreams and many other financial matters. The key insight he gained, which he shares in this book, is what works and what doesn't.

The Money Plan lays out what works. Experience taught Warren to keep financial advice simple and clear. It must be a reference people can carry around in their heads without it feeling like a burden. By breaking his Money Plan into five one-word stages (almost verbs really) he does this. And within each stage he lays out the logical steps you need to fulfill the goal of that stage. It will read – and feel – like commonsense. The reason: the basics of good money management involves reasonable actions that every one of us knows intuitively are right. Warren also knows that if people understand what you, as a financial advisor, are saying, they are more comfortable, open and empowered. Their goals become ones they can both articulate and achieve – with a workable plan and reasonable ongoing self-discipline.

Not everyone's financial needs and objectives will be the same. However, once you understand a few basic, time-tested strategies, you can adapt them, vary them to your specific needs. I use the word 'needs' here to include the emotions that you need to stay in control of in order to realise your money plan. Being your own bff – best financial friend – isn't only about mastering the numbers. It involves an awareness of what you find satisfying, what makes you happy, what removes worry, what motivates you. These are factors that underlie the goals you set in the very important Stage One of *The Money Plan*. I have long held that if you know the specific goal or goals you are working towards, like a comfortable, worry-free retirement, you increase your likelihood of achieving them. But part of setting your goals is making sure that the elements of your plan feel good and accomplishable to you. Knowing yourself is as important as knowing the numbers.

As I read the *The Money Plan* book I kept thinking back to the first time I met Warren Shute. It was 1998 when he was on my program *Investing for All with Alvin Hall*. Back then, while Warren had a clear sense of himself, he was still developing his own life plan – that is, how he would work in the financial services industry. Helping others was always one of the key components of his ambition and it has remained so over this 20-plus years as a financial advisor. Our early meeting developed into a friendship because Warren and I share values about honesty, integrity, kindness, truth, plain-talk and sharing. I have long believed in sharing my knowledge, experience and wisdom so that people can use it to make their financial lives better – in whatever ways are important to them. Warren Shute's *The Money Plan* is an inspiring manifestation of our shared philosophy. He's gained a tremendous amount of knowledge and wisdom over 20 years as a financial advisor. He now shares with you, the reader, what works. Now use his wise guidance to make a five-stage plan for yourself.

Alvin Hall
Financial educator, broadcaster and bestselling author

INTRODUCTION
Meeting Mr Planner

It was 9.55 on a wet Thursday morning in January. The cloud was low and the air damp. The gate buzzer rang – it was Mr and Mrs Peters arriving. They carefully reversed their BMW 3 Series Touring into the parking space and I could tell the type of clients they would be: careful and methodical.

My assistant brought their client profile into my office. I reclined in my chair, reading through each page carefully to get an understanding of the couple who were waiting in my reception and where on their journey of life they were right now.

Mr and Mrs Peters were in their early sixties, married with three children and two grandchildren. Mr Peters was looking to retire from a middle-management career with a manufacturing company and Mrs Peters was working part-time at a local library. As I scanned through their portfolio, I could hardly believe my eyes. Their net worth statement was incredible.

I learnt early on in my career that the power of our questions shapes our lives. Asking great questions gives us deep and meaningful relationships with ourselves and others. Questions guide our thoughts and therefore our decisions.

To be effective as a financial planner, I needed to know what was important to Mr and Mrs Peters, politely challenge their thoughts, make them a little uncomfortable in order for them to have a breakthrough – the 'aha' moment that I look for. As a Certified Financial Planner, I could then explain the territory and show how the sails could be adjusted to steer their financial plan in the direction of a smooth future.

Many people choose to eat healthily for what it gives them – a healthy, fit lifestyle. It's not because they prefer salmon and scrambled eggs over a bacon butty with brown sauce. Investing is the same. People invest because they want a happy, fruitful, secure future.

It's not because we enjoy making money – we enjoy what money can give us.

My question was, 'Welcome, Mr and Mrs Peters, I hope your journey here was safe and enjoyable. If we could achieve just one thing from today's meeting, what would it be?'

'We met you at the financial seminar you held in Cirencester, years ago,' Mrs Peters replied. 'We've been following what you taught ever since, and now feel we want to retire. We've finally decided to start the next chapter in our lives together. But we want to know if we have enough money.'

I talk a lot with my clients about the chapters in our lives and transitioning to the next chapter. We have different outcomes and objectives in each new chapter than we had in the previous one. Life is not one long road to infinity; it's a finite period of time. Our job is to fit as many experiences with as many people, places and things into this life as we can – to live like no one else.

'Let's look at your figures and add this up, shall we? You have your mortgage repaid?' I asked.

'Yes, we did this straight after we set up our emergency fund. You told us to split our snowball (see Section Four – Debt for more details on the snowball) and repay our debts and invest at the same time, so we did.'

'You have £20,000 saved in premium bonds?'

'Yes, our expenditure adds up to £2,000 per month, so we thought just over six months was fine.'

'You have stocks and shares ISAs of £110,000 each and pensions of £400,000 for you Mrs Peters and £800,000 for you Mr Peters. This totals £1.42m. That's great, congratulations.'

'When we came to your presentation, we were lost. We did not know what to do or how we were ever going to retire, but you made it so straightforward.'

The problem people have with change is habits. Habits make us and habits break us. Living the busy lives we have created for ourselves, we have become creatures of routine, and when we try to break this routine, we can so often fail.

Set yourself up for success by developing automatic rituals or routines that make the new way easy to follow. If you have ever thought of running a marathon, you could quite easily be put off by the distance, especially if you're not a runner. But if you start with baby steps – small, achievable steps that take you in the right direction – you're far more likely to succeed.

Be kind to yourself and celebrate your wins. No one is perfect – you're a human with imperfections. These imperfections make up your unique character.

This journey, which you will embark on with me by your side, will sometimes be challenging, sometimes difficult, but when you are moving towards your True North, your purpose, things are always that little bit easier.

Just like dieting, budgeting may work in the short-term, but as humans we don't like the restrictions that dieting places on us.

Most people massively underestimate how much they need to save for their retirement and fail to plan. They set off in their career and cruise into the ocean of life, knowing they will hit the land of retirement someday, but not knowing where this will be, or when. This is evidenced by the growing number of baby boomers in the UK who are retiring with debt and being forced into bankruptcy in their golden years.

Generally, my clients' interest in retirement planning starts when they reach their late forties and onwards, sometimes into their sixties. Before this age they may contribute to a pension, but it's like drinking a diet drink and saying they're on a diet while they eat burger and chips. Other financial distractions take priority, such as holidays, paying back student debt, home purchases, and for some, education fees. I appreciate and respect this. In addition, the buy now, pay later culture is an epidemic across the world, not just a UK problem.

Worldwide savings rates are scarily low; people just don't save any more. A survey by the Money Advice Service found that four in ten adults in the UK do not have more than £500 in savings*. Another survey by ING Bank suggests 28% of UK adults have nothing at all in the bank.

These statistics explain why bankruptcies among over sixty-fives rose by 470% between 2001 and 2011 to 1,972 people a year, the Debt Advice Foundation figures show.

*(moneyadviceservice.org.uk/en/corporate/four-out-of-10-adults-are-not-in-control-of-their-finances-new-strategy-launched-to-improve-uks-financial-capability).

These aren't high-risk entrepreneurs building a business; they are normal people. Bankruptcy is a chronic illness mainly caused by the lack of financial education and, sometimes, misfortune.

The size of debts has also increased; an over fifty-five borrower has 36% more unsecured debt than two years ago, according to the insurer Aviva. These are serious figures, where the typical retiree with unsecured debt now owes £23,188, up from £22,401 this time last year.

But why should people bother to save when they only get peanuts in interest? Because we are not saving for growth, we are saving for security. The amounts people save vary across the country. When people hear their friends and neighbours are saving, going without certain toys or pleasures, by osmosis it influences them in their decision process to do the same. Almost the opposite of keeping up with the Joneses. Too often people buy things they don't want, to impress people they don't know. Deep down, we are all birds of a feather.

I think the big problem in today's society is financial education. We're not taught at any time how to manage money, unless we're studying to be a finance director or accountant, and even they can find it a challenge managing their own money. It's a feature of the system failing society.

> ## We are overfed on information, but starved for knowledge.
>
> John Naisbitt

Our education system, as brilliant as it is, has not equipped us and isn't equipping our children with the knowledge of how to earn, save and invest money. I am passionate about financial education for children and I have worked in this area for some time. If we teach children the foundations of nutrition, we can then hope they'll make better dietary decisions. Similarly, if we teach children the foundations of money, we can expect them to make informed financial decisions as they mature into adulthood.

The average salary in the UK for the tax year ending 5 April 2015 was £27,600. This is a median average salary and an increase of 1.6% over the 2014 median average salary which was £27,200. These averages are for full-time employees with data taken from the ONS (Office for National Statistics) Annual Average Salary Survey. So if you earn an average salary from eighteen to state retirement age, you'll have earned over £1,380,000 in your working career – assuming no payrises! That's a massive amount of money.

Later in the book, I'll show you proven and tested methods I have used over the last twenty years as a financial planner to help clients with incomes of £10,000 p.a. to over £1m p.a.

As my father taught me:

It's not how much you have coming in that counts, it's what you do with what you have coming in.

Money mastery is like good nutrition. There are some no-nos when you want to get in shape, but more often it's about how much we eat, rather than what we eat that counts. And with money it's not how much you have coming in, but what you do with the money you have coming in that counts.

There is more than one way to create wealth, just as there is more than one way to lose body fat, and we're going to focus on the best way, not the quickest, newest or most trendy. We're going to focus on the way that's worked for me for twenty years.

You create your own financial security; society owes you nothing. The British government had, as of Quarter One of 2015, £1.56 trillion of debt, or 81.58% of its total income (Gross Domestic Production). The cost of servicing this debt amounts to around £43 billion each year, which is roughly 3% of GDP. Due to the government's significant budget deficit of c. £69 billion (its overspending), the national debt is increasing by approximately £73.5 billion per annum, or around £1.4 billion each week. This overspending, as much as you and I will be affected, needs to stop.

Maybe the government should read *David Copperfield* by Charles Dickens, written in 1850.

> **Annual income twenty pounds, annual expenditure nineteen [pounds] nineteen [shillings] and six [pence], result happiness. Annual income twenty pounds, annual expenditure twenty pounds ought and six, result misery.**
>
> Charles Dickens, David Copperfield

If you're reading this at a young age, you have the advantage of time on your side. When it comes to investing, time is definitely your friend. Albert Einstein once said that compound interest is the eighth wonder of the world: 'He who understands it, earns it, he who doesn't pays it'. But you also need pure grit and determination, powerful drivers to move you towards your goals.

Think back to when you were at school. If you were asked to do a project over the summer holiday and hand it in on the first day back, did you start with good intentions? But when did you actually finish it? For me, it was the week before I needed to go back to school. I did whatever it took to ensure it was finished on time. Then I was desperate, determined and definitely motivated; I didn't want to stay behind after school, doing it there.

If you've been around the block and feel you've left things too late, don't write yourself off. Focus on the actions you need and develop a plan with me. You may need to work a little longer than you'd hoped, but at least you'll have a plan, not a wish. Create financial independence – independence from working. Even if you enjoy your job, it may not be there to support you when you need it. Financial independence gives you choices, and only you can achieve it. Nobody can give it to you.

Most people moan about the state pension, and the biggest gripe seems to be how the government keeps changing the rules. Ministers tinker with it as if it's their money and not ours. There have been so many changes to the state pension over the years, they could fill a book in their own right.

The main problem is the increasing of the state retirement age. Now this is particularly important for the younger readers, as there has been talk for some time that the state retirement age will rise to seventy. Wow, this will help with your retirement income – the ONS published a report on 23 September 2015 that a newborn baby boy would expect to live 79.1 years and a newborn baby girl 82.8 years if mortality rates remain the same as they were in the UK in 2013–2015, so that means a male could work his whole life for nine years of retirement.

> **I don't think of work as work and play as play. It's all living.**
> Richard Branson

I believe that in life, we should either follow our passions and make work and our passions integrate, or make sure we earn enough money not to have to work as often, or for as long as most people do, so we can spend more time enjoying our passions. Life is not a continuum, we are here to live. Which will you choose?

Many people face an 'income shock' when they retire. British workers earn an average of £27,600 a year but the basic state pension is just £8,296.60 a year for a single person (source: www.gov.uk).

The average private pension pot (not income) is worth just £10,000, according to Phoenix, the pension fund manager. This sum would produce an annual income for a sixty-five-year-old man of only £300 pa.

> **The only thing you deserve is what you earn.**
> **Tom Brands**

So, anyone in this position would see their income fall on retirement by more than 68%, or about £19,003 a year. A scary thought. That means on Retirement Day Number One, rather than live the life they want, they'll need to live the life they have got.

Of course, there'll be options, but life is a ticking clock and we need to take massive action to sort this out. Take control and head towards a happy, healthy, long-term retirement, rather than the road to misery and 'getting-by'.

Working longer and retiring later may be your only option. It is now easier to work beyond state retirement age because the default retirement age has been scrapped. Employers are now not allowed to dispense with your services simply because of your age, although they can make you retire if they can show that your age makes it impossible for you to do your job adequately. We need to play the cards we're dealt, but no one is out of the game. I will show you how to take back control of your finances and regain your self-respect.

I love work. I work a lot, but I work a lot less than I did in my twenties and thirties, and I know I will be working even less in ten years from now. I keep myself physically and mentally fit and healthy. I work out and watch what I eat, but age changes everyone's physical energies and values. Where we may want to work twelve to fourteen hours a day in our twenties, later in life family and personal time become more important. We change, things change. My aim is for you to be in control of your financial wellbeing to make the choices you want, not the ones you need.

> **My aim is for you to be financially independent of your business, not financially dependent on it.**

The best time to start planning for your future was yesterday. The second best time is now. So, unless you're Marty McFly, the best we can work with is where you are today.

Fear not. We have the tools and solutions within the book to show you how to do this. It will mean changing your habits, so it may be uncomfortable at first, but you can do it. Most people in the world can walk because when they were babies, their parents/guardians didn't say, 'Oh, what a shame, he/she is not a walker,' and give up. Their parents picked them up and got them to try again and again until they did walk.

That's what we're going to do over the course of this book. I'm going to share with you a proven system that works. Keep working it until you succeed, like many people have before you, and set yourself up for financial mastery.

STAGE ONE
GOALS

CHAPTER 1
What's Your Why?

Tony Robbins said, 'Successful people ask better questions, and as a result, they get better answers.'

A favourite question of mine is:

How do you want to spend the rest of your life?

When you look into the future – next year, three years, five years and ten years from now – do you like where you're heading?

Knowing where to start is often the biggest hurdle. But realising you need to make a change is a great first step. If you're lacking motivation to make the change, you need to get so uncomfortable with where you are today that change becomes an absolute must. Look at your reasons why. Why do you want to change? Magnify these reasons; make them so compelling they excite or scare you.

A proven plan will get you started, no matter where you're coming from, where you are now, or where you're going. There's no better time than right now to make a plan and get on track.

When our values are aligned, we have happiness.

For over twenty years, I have helped individuals develop plans to put them on a track for happiness. People don't want £1m; they can't eat it, cuddle it or get pleasure from it. They want what money will give them.

Our values in life are what are important to us, so if we align our financial plan with our values, we will by default achieve happiness. We have a choice to take charge of our future, or allow others to take charge of it for us. We either live our life, or someone else's life. Which will it be?

> ## It's what money will provide that's important to us, not money itself.

What are your Values?

All people have certain values they believe in and live by. These are the innermost beliefs that distinguish who we are and how we conduct ourselves.

Values are things that are very important to us. They may include family, health, career, and spirituality. Having strong convictions about what we value, and keeping them front and centre, keeps us balanced and focused on the most important things in life. In the long run, focusing on what we value, coupled with a solid plan, will help us live a fulfilling life far more than any short-term gain from compromising will.

Having strong convictions benefits us in other ways, too. In times of indecision, we can turn to our guiding values. They will frequently give us the framework for making tough decisions. When we're unhappy, we can turn to our values and see if we're leading a life that is consistent with them. When we're underachieving, we can turn to our values and gain the motivation to make the extra effort.

Have you ever met someone who seems to have everything together? They are happy, calm and 'live purposely'? This is how we are when we understand and live our life in accordance with our values. Then our whole life is in a flow; we know why we are doing what we are doing.

To find out what your values are, ask yourself the following question and write down the answer. Repeat the question until you can no longer write down a response.

What is important to you in life?

When you can no longer write down an answer, you have finished. Look through the answers and ask yourself if each one is really true. Do any answers jump out as being more important than the others? Write the top five in order of importance.

These are likely to be your top five values in life. Now check decisions you have made against them. Write these values in your journal, or print them and keep them in a safe place for future reference. I keep mine on the reverse of my Compelling Vision; more on this later.

Decision making. Have you ever had trouble making a decision? In business and in life, we have to make decisions all the time. Many of them involve grey areas where more than one solution will work. These grey areas can lead to indecisiveness, which means you are not clear on your values. Once you bring clarity to your values, making decisions becomes easier.

Take this for an example: let's say it's important to you to spend time on your health. You want to be fit and strong and a role model for others, perhaps your children. Yet Saturday night comes along and your friends badger you to go out all night, drinking alcohol, eating pizza and partying.

Follow your Values

Follow your strongest values for a happier life. Your values are neither right, nor wrong; they are not what other people think they should be. They are whatever makes you happy in the long run.

Happiness

Far too many people in our society go through life without zest and enthusiasm. Frequently, this is because they are doing and being things that are not congruent with who they are. The result can be burnout, depression, and ineffectiveness.

The key is to evaluate what is important to you, and then make sure your life is in sync with that.

I have found that in order to be happy, I need to schedule 'me time' – time for me to do the things that are important in my life. It is all very well trying to be all things to all people, but true happiness comes from following your own values. This may require you to say 'no' more often than you currently do, which may take practice. Saying no does not mean you do not love or care for others in your life; it simply means that there is a vision that you want to achieve and work towards which is greater than you currently have.

Make your vision of the future so compelling, it excites you, gets you up early and keeps you up late.

There's a saying attributed to various people, from Albert Einstein to Tony Robbins. Whoever said it, it's true.

If you do what you've always done, you'll get what you've always got.

Decide on purpose what it is you want, align your future vision, your future self, with your values, and consistently take steps to work towards this.

Achievement

Some of the greatest achievements have come from people who were willing to devote their lives, and in some cases, sacrifice their lives, to live their values. The key is to feel so strongly about your values, you are motivated to take action. Having conviction about something you value, and then committing to live by it every single day, will go a long way towards igniting relentless burning desire.

For many people, this will be new territory – an area of their life which they have not explored to date. It may instil fear of the unknown. How could this possibly be true? How would this work? This lack of confidence is often a result of lack of previous experience or references. Remember, experiences can be gained by learning or reading as well as doing.

Your mind cannot decipher the difference between something that is experienced, or vividly imagined.

This is well-known in the scientific world. Think about a scary film or nightmare you may have experienced – it wasn't real, so why did you feel shocked or scared? Because your mind could not tell it wasn't real. This is why sports professionals do visualisation techniques along with physical activities to perfect their skills. If it works for them, it will work for you.

Take a moment to think of the first time you did something that you are now accomplished in. This could be learning a new skill, starting a new class, or maybe the beginning of a relationship with a friend or partner. If you're really struggling for an idea, decide now to learn something new to expand your horizon and grow as an individual. If you have so many examples it's hard to choose one, think of a clear, memorable experience.

How did you feel before you started the new skill? Before you went to the class on your first day? Before you got to know the new person in your life?

For most of us, if it's an early experience, there is apprehension, worry or even anxiety. The butterfly feeling in our stomach. What helps overcome these feelings is experiences of success – references to 'when I did this, it worked out OK'. If you're worried, it is probably because you are imagining a future possibility, or are thinking of an event that happened in the past and magnifying the worst parts.

> **We cannot be afraid if we bring our attention to the present moment. When we are worried or scared, we are either thinking of the past or creating the future.**

So here are my two top tips to increase your confidence to build the future you deserve:

1. **Spend most of your time, especially if you're in familiar surroundings, in the present moment.** The only place and the only time that matters is here, right now. This has been developed into the art of mindfulness, and there are dozens of brilliant books and sites devoted to it. But for now, bring your attention to this moment, while you read the words on this page, and enjoy being present.

Now, this may take practice. You may experience your mind wandering off, thinking of the things you need to do. I use the Evernote app on my smartphone to brain dump every distraction that comes up so I can let it go and remain present. You can use whatever suits you best.

2. **Honour self-promises and reward yourself with kindness.** What do I mean by that? When you say that you will do something, ensure that you follow through. This does not need to be a public declaration because we're honouring self-promises, not trying to raise our egos by competing with others. We are building self belief and self-confidence. When our values are aligned with our future vision and we honour our own self-promises, we live in harmony.

So, for example, when you say you are going to work out (walk in the morning, go to the gym, do a yoga class), do it. If someone asks you to do something different, say you can't because you're honouring a self-promise. Hey, I realise we all have demands on our time, but we all have twenty-four hours in a day. How we invest those hours is our choice. We decide what it is that we want and take daily consistent actions towards achieving this.

I decide to wake early in the morning and have what I refer to as my hour of power. The first thing I do is drink some water. I then open my journal and write:

● Five actions I want to achieve that day, because when I have decided on them, not the distractions of the day, I am setting myself up for a successful day

- Three things that happened yesterday to review them, congratulate myself, build confidence and learn from any mistakes

- Three things I am grateful for to remain humble in this wonderful life I have developed

- A few lines of journaling to allow myself to clear my mind

Once I have done this, and it takes me about ten to fifteen minutes, I meditate. I vary my meditation, because I want to keep things fresh and new. Routine helps us to achieve more, but it can stifle our passion for life.

I generally sit in a chair when I meditate, looking outside. I listen to either some light meditation music, or my own compilation, which I have on my site for download at www.WarrenShute.com/TheMoneyPlan/BrainTraining. I meditate for fifteen minutes, sometimes longer, sometimes not as long, but I rarely do fewer than ten minutes.

Then I work out for no more than thirty minutes. I train six days a week, only resting on a Sunday, alternating weights and cardio.

After my workout, I am done. This is my hour of power, to myself, for myself.

One hour to yourself each day is just 4% of your day.

Purpose

We all have certain desires and pursuits in life, such as ensuring our security and caring for loved ones. But, when you move beyond the day-to-day pursuits of life, what moves you? What causes you to jump out of bed in the morning, feeling refreshed and ready to tackle the day's challenges? What higher purpose calls you? What is something larger than yourself that inspires you? What can you do that uses all your skills, talents, and interests, and benefits the world?

Without a meaningful purpose, we simply go through the motions of daily life. We respond to the alarm clock, go to work, solve the day's problems, eat, relax, spend a few minutes with the family, go to bed, and then we wake up and do it all over again. We could do that for fifty years, and then look back on what we've accomplished and be sadly disappointed.

Each of us is capable of making a positive impact in the life we live. For many people, being a loving spouse and raising great kids is a huge accomplishment, and they should be rightfully proud of that. However, meaningful purpose transcends what we do for ourselves and our immediate family. Meaningful purpose reaches out to the world around us and infuses life with the special gifts each of us has inside.

I believe we have chapters in our lives where we move from one defining period to another. Now everyone's periods are unique depending on their life decisions, and they can be micro level (a year or two in each period, so life has many 'chapters'), or larger periods.

On the larger scale, I feel we all have three main chapters in our life:

- Childhood (birth to twenty-one)
- Adulthood or working life (twenty-one to sixty-six)
- Retirement (sixty-six to our final days)

And obviously within these chapters there are many smaller defining periods. Once we are a young adult, say twenty-one, we have approximately forty-five years before we retire – bear with me, I appreciate we are all individual. Actuarially, we may live to eighty-eight, so forty-five years working is approximately 50% of our life on this wonderful planet.

So, our life can broadly be split into:

- Childhood – 25%

- Adulthood – 50%

- Retirement – 25%

If we use all our childhood to prepare for our adulthood, and if we use all our adulthood to make our retirement fun, we're missing 50%–75% of our life. Why am I telling you this? Because in my twenty-plus years as a financial planner, I have seen hundreds of clients planning for retirement as if adulthood is a preparation ground. It's not. It's all called life, and we need to ensure we are extracting the juice from it.

There is far too much unconscious living going on in our world today, where we are transfixed by someone else's agenda, going along with the flow and numbing our feelings, be it with excess alcohol, food, or other forms of addiction.

Promise yourself you will learn what your higher purpose is. What do you truly love to do? Then find a way to achieve this. It may not come immediately, but by allowing yourself 'me time', you will ensure it will come to you. As a child, you may have wanted to be an astronaut, fireman or nurse. What is it you want now?

> **If you don't know where you are going,
> any road will get you there.**
>
> Lewis Carroll, Alice in Wonderland

People of great achievement know exactly where they're going, and they take the necessary steps to get there. But where is 'there' for you? 'There' is your ideal future scenario, your future vision.

> **What goals would you be setting for
> yourself if you knew you could not fail?**
>
> Robert H. Schuller

This question has been a guiding force for me throughout my life. What is it you would do now? Why don't you pursue this? What's stopping you?

You may want to be a professional footballer, but do you really want to be a professional footballer, or do you just enjoy playing football? If it's the latter, why not play more football? Or get involved more with football?

You may want to run your own charity. Why not get more involved in charitable causes to build your knowledge and experience and move this way?

George Kinder is a Harvard educated financial planner, philosopher, mindfulness teacher, author, and the founder of the Kinder Institute of Life Planning, an organisation that has trained over 3,000 professionals in 30 countries in what is considered the gold standard for adviser-client relationship skills. George has written six books including the *Seven Stages of Money Maturity*, in which you can find the following three questions (or online at LifePlanningForYou.com, a free consumer online Life Planning website).

Imagine you are financially secure; that you have enough money to take care of your needs, now and in the future. How would you live your life? Would you change anything? Let yourself go. Don't hold back on your dreams. Describe a life that is completely and richly yours.

Now imagine that you visit your doctor, who tells you that you have only five to ten years to live. You won't ever feel sick, but you will have no notice of the moment of your death. What will you do in the time you have remaining? Will you change your life and how will you do it? (Note that this question does not assume unlimited funds.)

Finally, imagine that your doctor shocks you with the news that you only have twenty-four hours to live. Notice what feelings arise as you confront your very real mortality. Ask yourself, 'What did I miss? Who did I not get to be? What did I not get to do?'

These are very powerful questions which, if you take the time to answer them, will help you understand what your true purpose and compelling vision look like.

This material was developed by George Kinder and the Kinder Institute of Life Planning. It is part of a programme of trainings that lead to the Registered Life Planner® designation. Used by permission of George Kinder © 1999, 2009, 2017.

> ## The goal is to die with memories, not dreams.
> **Tiny Buddha**

Your vision for your environmental surroundings, the people you associate with, what you spend your time doing, and what you want to accomplish is different to everybody else's. For example, perhaps you want to be successfully self-employed, working from home, and living in the Cotswolds. Or, perhaps you want to work for a charity that speaks to your heart and live near your children and grandchildren. It can be anything, but it must be something, and it must be clearly defined. It must include tangibles so you can see it, feel it, touch it, smell it, and hear it. Get all your senses involved in helping you drive towards it. The clearer and more specific your vision, the more you will believe in it.

Your vision must be compelling. It must be something that motivates you to jump out of bed in the morning and get working. It is what will sustain you when the going gets tough and you face obstacles. To develop it, disengage from the present and position yourself in a future with unlimited possibilities. Eliminate your limiting beliefs and think big. With this frame of mind, you can develop a vision that propels you to success, contribution, and happiness far beyond what you've ever imagined.

Create a compelling vision to take action towards the life you want.

Here's an example of a compelling vision of the future: 'I enthusiastically jump out of bed every morning full of love for God, family, friends, and life. I am a husband my wife is proud of, a father my children look up to, and a friend people count on.'

Summary

- Remember, it's the power of your questions that shape your destiny. If you want a better future, ask better questions

- We have three broad chapters in our life, childhood taking up 25%, adulthood taking 50% and retirement taking 25%. Don't waste the first 75% just to enjoy the home straight

- Honour self-promises and reward yourself with kindness

- Elicit your values and list them in order of priority to you

- Write your Compelling Future and make sure it resonates with you

- Print and laminate your values, goals (covered in the next chapter) and vision, and read them when you wake and before you retire at night

CHAPTER 2
Goal Setting

The distance between your dreams and reality is called discipline

Traditionally, goal setting has not been a British thing to do. However, I have grown up on it. With an American father and an early exposure to Tony Robbins, I have consistently set myself goals to work towards to guide my life.

It is my belief that if we are not living our own goals, we will be living someone else's. If we don't have any goals to direct our life and we get up in the morning, pour ourselves a cup of our favourite coffee, go to work nine to five, come home and watch Netflix, we are living to support the producer of our favourite coffee's goal to become number 1 in the UK, our boss's goals in running his or her company, and Netflix's goal of global entertainment domination.

Make your life a choice. Decide how you want to spend the rest of your life, set your goals and work towards these.

We all have wants and desires. We can all daydream about what it would be like to be living our ideal life. Unfortunately, despite what *The Secret* book may say, merely thinking about our ideal life will not get us our ideal life. We have to be clear about what we want, when we want it, why we want it, and we have to take positive action to make it happen – put some work into it.

For example, if we merely go out into the garden and say, 'There are no weeds, there are no weeds, there are no weeds,' the damn weeds will come and take over. We must have a goal (which is a target objective or outcome we want), then we must take action towards achieving this goal, periodically check in with our progress (reassess as we go along), and continue taking action until we achieve our goal.

Please note I said *continue* taking action *until* we achieve our goal.

The goal setting process is critical to making all this happen. As we set goals, we must make sure they are SMAC certified.

SMAC is an acronym for:

- Specific
- Measurable
- Achievable
- Compatible

One of the keys to goal setting is to tie them into your compelling vision. Your compelling vision is a lifetime pursuit. To make it manageable, break it into pieces. To do this, complete the goal setting and action planning exercises that you can download from WarrenShute.com/ TheMoneyPlan/Goals.

As you set goals, start by reviewing your compelling vision and then work backwards. To pursue your vision, what has to happen in ten years, five years, three years and one year? Determine what age you, your spouse and your children will be at each of those time periods. Identify the goal, then determine *the one activity* that will have the greatest impact on reaching that goal. Also, identify the reward you will get by reaching the goal.

We need to write our goals out because it clarifies them for us and sticks a flag in the ground to say, 'This is where I am now, this is what I am moving towards'.

Don't make your goals a moving target, or you'll find it hard to hit them.

I don't believe in the old adage that if you share your goals with others, you are more likely to achieve them. It's a personal choice. If you share your goals with others, you may not want them to see you as a failure, so you will do whatever it takes to complete the goal. On the other hand, you may not want the additional pressure which sharing brings.

However, what is important is to read your goals every night before you go to sleep and every morning upon awakening. This will keep them in the forefront of your mind and significantly increase the odds of you achieving them. You will literally be programming your brain for success.

I have laminated my compelling vision and goals and put a copy by my bed. I take a copy with me when I travel and I have also put a copy on the mirror in my gym, but this could just as easily be put in my journal.

When you shine a torch with a wide beam, the light fades, but it spreads over a wider area. When you bring the spread of light in and laser focus the beam, it can cut through steel. Why am I sharing this with you? I want you to be as specific as possible. Have a few goals, no more than two to three in each area. Having laser attention on these will increase your probability of success.

So, let's work with this:

● You have established your values, and ranked these so you know your top five values in life

● You have your compelling vision

Your goals might be:

Bigger picture – where I'm heading over ten years. Financially independent of working; spending my time with my spouse and family.

Check in point – five years. Repaid mortgage. Maximum funding pension. Be home from work by 6pm and family time at weekends.

Check in point – three years. Complete unsecured debt repayment. Finish additional training at work and seek promotion.

Laser focus – one year. Get financially organised. Save £1,000. Start debt repayment plan.

Now, twelve months is a long period of time and life gets in the way. So we need check-ins throughout the year.

Many people make New Year resolutions – what are these if not goals? But what happens to most New Year resolutions? They are forgotten by 1 February. That's why we have a plan to track them, keeping them in the forefront of our mind and checking in to see how we're doing.

I want you to check in every three months. I call these 90 Day Check-ins, which are meaningful steps along the road to success.

> **The difference between who you are and who you want to be is what you do.**
> **Bill Phillips**

90-Day Check-ins

I often speak of rocks and pebbles, rocks being the big, important items in life and pebbles the smaller things. Pebbles are often prettier than large rocks, but rocks are heavy, sturdy and necessary. Focus on the rocks in life, the important targets for achievement, and let the pebbles fit in around your rocks.

Timeframe	Goal Board
Ten-year vision	Financially independent of working, spending my time with my spouse and family.
Five-year vision	Debt free. Maximum funding pension. Be home from work at 6pm and family time at weekends.
Three-year vision	Complete unsecured debt repayment. Finish exams and study to gain promotion and pay rise at work.
One-year vision	Save £1,000 emergency fund and repay £1,500 of debt. Get financially organised (Bank Account System). Spend within my WAM (Walk About Money). Get a second income. Share with others what I am doing.
90-Day Check-in Q1	Put £500 into savings account. Open up a WAM Account. Draw up a shortlist of second job options. Join the WarrenShuteCFP Facebook group.
90-Day Check-in Q2	Save a further £500, so I have £1,000 in savings account. Give myself a pat on the back for using the Bank Account System. Set up second income job/apply for positions.
90-Day Check-in Q3	Repay £500 of debt using the snowball method. Share with friends what I have done – pay it forward. Put any additional money from second income towards paying off debt.
90-Day Check-in Q4	Repay £500 of debt from pay, plus £500 from second income. Support others in the WarrenShuteCFP Facebook group.

90-Day Check-ins are quarterly targets which you need to work towards to achieve your yearly goals.

Print yours out, laminate them if possible and put them by the side of your bed. To this day, I still read my goals and Check-ins every night before I turn out my light and every morning before I work out.

Remember SMAC. Don't try to do everything in a quarter.

> **Most people overestimate what they can do in one year and underestimate what they can do in ten years.**
>
> **Bill Gates**

You can go to WarrenShute.com/TheMoneyPlan/Goals to download a template to complete and FaceBook.com/WarrenShuteCFP to join the Facebook group for ongoing support.

Summary

- Don't make your goals a moving target, or you'll find it hard to hit them

- Review your 90-Day Check-ins frequently – daily, or at least a few times a week

- Create your Goal Board – write your ten-year, five-year and three-year visions, and your twelve-month goals

- Write your action steps to achieve your twelve-month goals – your 90-Day Check-in

- Laminate and read your goals daily

- Join the Facebook Group Facebook.com/ WarrenShuteCFP

CHAPTER 3
Set Yourself Up For Financial Success

We are emotional beings in a physical body. What do I mean by that? We are run by our emotions. Even people who are logical and rational support their thinking processes with the emotions their thoughts create.

Tony Robbins established that we have six human needs, or driving forces. I have linked these to financial wellbeing over the years, and I want to highlight them to explain that when we understand the rules, we can win the game of money.

Certainty

The first of the human needs, the emotions that we crave, is certainty. We all need an element of certainty in our life – certainty that we will wake up in the morning; certainty that when we drive down the street, the oncoming car will stay in its lane. This feeling of certainty also works in the financial world. By building an emergency fund, we increase our feeling of certainty, and we are more certain than we were that we can succeed. By repaying our unsecured debts, we are building a stronger financial future, stronger foundations. And ultimately, when we build our critical mass of investment capital, we provide certainty of income for our future.

Variety or uncertainty

Now, even though humans crave a level of certainty, we also need variety or uncertainty or we'd get bored out of our minds. This is, in my opinion, the reason why most people never achieve financial freedom – getting wealthy can be boring!

The secret of success in many areas of life is to get a system, work it and make it automatic or habitual. Fat loss is a great example. Find an evidence-backed eating programme that works for you, get yourself a training programme, follow the programme consistently over weeks, months and years to achieve the physique you desire.

Oops, where is the instant gratification? Years? I want that physique now!

The reason most people fail to lose weight, and fail to become wealthy, is because the programme only works when the basics are done well and consistently, and this is the opposite of the human desire for variety. Consistency is boring. Variety can be exciting and often variety wins because as humans we do wants over shoulds or musts – 'I want that cake/glass of wine/burger even though I know I shouldn't.'

Significance

The third human need is significance. When I say significance, this is not necessarily ego. Why do people stand in line overnight to buy the latest iPhone? Is it really that different to the previous model? Because their 'identity' revolves around being the first. The significance of owning the latest model drives them to stand in line.

For some, it's the latest or most expensive car, watch, suit or qualification. For others, significance comes from charitable endeavours or raising the perfect child.

If you find your significance comes from being a consumer of goods (iPhones, watches, cars) and you establish this needs to change because it's preventing you from achieving your desired future lifestyle, work on changing your mindset to become an owner of the goods instead. If you had invested £500 into Apple stock on the release date of each of the previous ten models, starting in 2007, you would have invested £5,000 in total. In September 2017, you would have had £116,000 – a gain of more than £110,000 in ten years.

> **Change your mindset to become an owner rather than a consumer and change your financial destiny.**

Connection or love

The fourth human need is connection or love, which can work antagonistically with significance. As human beings, we need an element of connection and love with others. Some people need it with things, e.g. a smartphone. Some people will give you anything as giving provides them with the dopamine boost that makes them feel good. If you relate to this and regularly give away more money than you have, work on ways to give to others in a different way. I want you to give, but I will teach you how to make more money so you have a lot to give rather than a little. The old adage goes, 'Give a man a fish, feed him for a day. Teach a man to fish, feed him for his life.' Become a teacher of fishing, rather than a giver of fish.

If you give too much, too soon, you may end up becoming a liability to the ones you love. Secure your finances, secure your future.

Growth

Growth is the fifth human need, which feeds our desire for improvement and development. Some of us have a greater growth need than others. My growth need is very big, for example – I love to learn and improve. It's in every cell of my body.

Take pride in your accomplishments, in your achievements. Reward yourself and be kind to yourself. You're a precious human being.

Contribution

Contribution is the sixth human need. To contribute towards society is what makes us human. It makes us alive. Consciously give and share to feel wealthy.

When you give, this can be in the form of money, time, ideas or love. As your wealth builds, tithing to your favourite charity or cause can bring happiness to both sides. I know that may seem silly, but 10% of £100 is easier for many to give than 10% of £1m.

Giving is the key to true happiness.

Great people of our time are givers. A mentor of mine, Bill Phillips, is a significant donor to the Make a Wish foundation. Tony Robbins gave all the proceeds of his recent *Money Master the Game* book to charity, and Martin Lewis, founder of Money Saving Expert, very generously gave £10m of the £87m sale proceeds to good causes when he sold moneysavingexpert.co.uk.

Pay it forward, live abundantly and give consciously.

Summary

- We are emotional beings in a physical body. Our emotions are our operating system

- We need to plan and work for financial success; it doesn't happen by accident

- Progressing financially provides certainty

- The process of becoming wealthy can be boring: be prepared

- Become an owner rather than a consumer

- Pay it forward

STAGE TWO
HOW TO GET FINANCIALLY ORGANISED

CHAPTER 4
The Bank Account System

This book is an action book. For best results, you need to take action – implement the strategies I'm sharing as you go through the book, improve your financial wellbeing, re-read the parts you didn't quite get, and join our Facebook community at facebook.com/WarrenShuteCFP. Ask us questions. Own it.

Section Two is all about how to get financially well organised.

Many people who come to see me struggle with the basics of money management. The day-to-day management of money is essential for a happy life – ask anyone who is in debt.

We've already established that we'll work for about 50% of our life and spend what we save during this time on the last 25%. Earning an average wage from eighteen to state retirement age means we'll have over £1 million passing through our bank account during our lifetime. That's a massive amount of money. But whether you earn £10,000 or £1 million a year, the principles of managing money are the same.

The Bank Account System I developed with my clients has successfully been used now for over twenty years. I believe that if we can make the day-to-day operations of our finances automatic, we stand a higher chance of financial success.

Here's how it works. There are a couple of variants, depending on whether you are single or keep your finances separate, or share your income and expenditure.

If you are employed or self-employed/a business owner, your income is likely to be paid to you on a calendar month basis. However, if it is not, that's no problem - you can either pay it into the Reserve Account when it falls due or adapt the following to suit your circumstances.

The Bank Account System

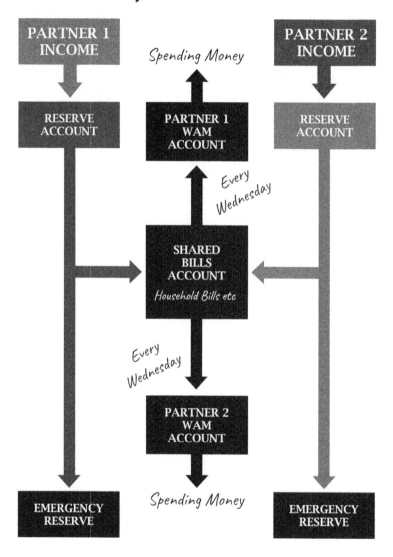

If you prefer to keep your income separate from your spouse/partner, when you are paid your income will be paid into the Reserve Account. If you prefer to combine your money, your income can be paid directly into the Bills Account and you can miss the Reserve Account out altogether. Treat the Reserve Account as a form of holding account.

Bills Account

If you have decided to use a Reserve Account, each month automatically transfer sufficient funds to your Bills Account (usually the same amount each month) to cover your regular bills. All of your regular committed payments will be made from this account. These payments include your Emergency Reserve account savings, rent/mortgage, utilities, phone, WAM (see below), children's pocket money (if applicable), holiday account savings, minimum debt repayment (if applicable) and snowball overpayment/ investment etc. – anything which is regular in nature. They will all be paid by direct debit or standing order – automatically.

Now, go through each payment one by one and ask yourself:

- Do I need this payment?
- Do I want this payment?
- Can I buy a similar experience for less?

Be ruthless. The more you can realistically cut your expenditure, the more surplus you will have to use to repay your debts and invest. The intention with this exercise is for you to find missing pounds.

WAM (Walk About Money)

WAM is the money you use on incidentals which are not covered under the recurring payments from the Bills Account. So, this would include things like a cappuccino from the local coffee shop, a haircut, fuel for your car, online payments, 'Friday night' money…anything and everything that you spend on a weekly basis is covered by your WAM.

Each week, on a Wednesday, automatically transfer your weekly 'allowance' or WAM money from your Bills Account to your WAM Account by standing order. I say Wednesday because from research, I know most of my clients' spending occurs at a weekend (when they are not working), so the funds will be in their account ready. Once the weekend is over, there are only two days to wait before they are paid WAM money again.

So between your WAM Account and your Bills Account *all of your spending* should be covered and automated.

I said weekly for a reason, because once this money is spent, seven days is not long to wait to receive another dopamine boost payment. When we are paid monthly, restricting our spending for a whole month is like holding our breath or saying, 'I'm going without any cheat food in my diet for sixteen weeks' – we can do it, but it's difficult.

I don't believe budgets work. A budget is like a diet. Psychologically, when we say no to something our brain often wants it more than ever. Think about your favourite food (mine is pizza). If I went on a diet where I could never have pizza, I'd last all of a few days. However, if I decided to eat pizza in a controlled manner, say once a week, and the rest of the time I ate well, I'd have taken the 'never' out of the equation. I'd be eating through choice, not restriction.

So rather than say, 'I must not buy this, that or the other', look at spending money like calories. We all have a TDEE (Total Daily Energy Expenditure) which is the number of calories our body uses to function and move. This is our baseline. When we regularly consume calories in excess of our TDEE, we gain weight in the form of fat. It's the same with money. We have an 'allowance' (our WAM) that we can spend. When we spend in excess of this allowance, we use our reserves and get financially fat, i.e. in debt.

OK, so we know when to pay ourselves, but how much WAM do we pay? If we have debt or if we're not on track financially, we need to cut back on our excesses. Cut back, not eliminate. If we went from eating 4,000 calories per day to 1,800, we'd be unlikely to last. We need to manage our financial expenditure.

List all the things that you buy personally (not by direct debit or standing order) on a weekly or monthly basis, include the following:

- Fuel or transportation

- Meals out and lunches

- Coffees and snacks

- Entertainment such as cinema, drinks with friends and takeaways

- Haircuts, beauty treatments and massages

- Amazon and online purchases

- Clothes and gifts

- Groceries and supplements

- Club payments

Take a look at your current spending statements and review what you spend. Include everything. Once you have grouped your expenditure together, ask yourself these questions:

● Do I need to buy this in future?

● Do I want to buy this in future?

● Can I buy a similar experience for less?

Now add up your revised expenditure, using the reduced figures. Can you cut this spending by 10% and stick to it? This is the balancing act – the more you reduce your spending, the quicker you'll repay your debt and be financially free. However, if you go too wild here, you won't succeed.

Watch and feedback to yourself how it's going. Remember, we're playing the long game.

This is a plan for life, not the next three weeks.

I want you to succeed, so use these tricks to set yourself up for success.

So what about if you have debt? What about if your car breaks down? What about holidays? I will cover the repayment of debt in a later chapter when we discuss the snowball repayment method, but for the purposes of this chapter, the minimum card and loan payments, plus the snowball payment (the additional payment covered in Section Four – Debt), must be included as a regular bill payment being automatically paid from the Bills Account. So your monthly minimum card payments will be set up, usually by direct debit, and your snowball overpayment will be a separate additional standing order payment.

Emergency Payments
What's covered under emergency payments? Car breakdowns, dental bills – any emergencies which are not accounted for elsewhere and are a one-off payment that must be made. These are covered from your Emergency Reserve Account. To start with, if you still have unsecured debt, this will contain £1,000 (or a greater amount if you feel it's necessary).

Start your Emergency Reserve Account at £1,000 and use any spare money you have to repay high cost unsecured debt. Once the debt is gone, build this account up to cover six months of your expenditure. If you need to draw down and use this account, your first action step afterwards will be to replenish it back to £1,000 (or six months' worth of expenditure) before paying any further debt.

For example, you have £1,000 in your Emergency Reserve Account and you have £10,000 of unsecured debt, of which you are paying £100 pm minimum payment and a further £150 pm snowball payment. If you need to use your Emergency Reserve Account for an unexpected car bill of £300, you would immediately stop the snowball payment of £150 pm (keep the minimum £100 pm payment going) and replenish the £300 emergency fund deficit over the next two months, before returning to the snowball repayment.

Two things here are vital. Firstly, always maintain at least the minimum payment. Secondly, replenish the Emergency Reserve as soon as you can.

Holidays
Holidays should be priced into the monthly payments. For example, if you intend to spend £2,400 pa on a family holiday, you would include in your monthly Bills Account a payment for £200 pm. Open a separate account and call it Holiday Account and transfer the £200 into it automatically each month.

When you do this, remember you may need access to the money before the day you go away – you'll need to pay for things in advance, so ensure you divide the money needed by the months you have until you need the money.

This is the prefunding way of paying for a holiday. If you normally put holidays on a credit card then repay the credit card, I want you to get out of this habit. Use cash and save for the things you need.

Money to the Children

I have two wonderful children, Olly and Bella, and my wife Nicky and I enjoy raising them and teaching them lessons for their life. I have no plan for my children's lives other than that they pursue a passion that excites them and contributes to society.

I am unable to keep count of the number of wealthy children who have inherited money or assets from family members, or won money, only to have spent it all a few years later. A significant amount of first generation wealth is lost by the second generation, and an even larger amount is lost by the third generation. Financial education needs to start at home.

I have worked with many of my clients' children and I have taught in schools. We can make money fun and engaging. Children don't need a PhD in finance; they need to understand the basics. Many of us cannot explain how electricity works, but we're happy to use the light switch and know enough to avoid being electrocuted.

There are many opinions on whether we should give money to our children or get them to do chores for their money and earn it. Who knows which opinion is right?

Let me share what we do at home. As a parent, I believe we have a few significant responsibilities. We should teach our children manners, to contribute to society and to enjoy working.

Nicky and I decided to give an allowance to our children and link this allowance to their age. We give £2 per month for each year of their age. So when Olly turned twelve, he got £24 per month, and when Bella turned ten, she got £20 per month. In general, we pay for their needs (clothing, food, school trips, etc.) and they pay for their wants (gifts to friends and family, toys, sweets, etc.). We are teaching our children to manage money, understand budgeting and that once the money is spent, it's gone. We are teaching them to think about 'budgeting' in children's terms, confidence to buy things themselves and independence.

We still police certain purchases, as they may not have the ability to rationalise an expensive purchase, or understand that they may not get as much pleasure from it as they think, but we do this with them, not for them. They can each spend an amount equal to their age in pounds before they need to ask permission.

So, for example, at the time of writing, Olly is twelve. If he wanted to buy a game for £20, he'd need to check in with Nicky or myself to explain what he was doing and why. We'd test him to discover if he really needed or wanted it, and that it was at the best price he could find, then we'd either approve or say no to the purchase. It is good and natural for children to hear the word no occasionally.

We have certain expectations in the house which are not linked to the allowance. They have to keep the place tidy, not only their rooms, and offer to make drinks for everyone rather than just themselves. However, their job is to take out the rubbish and the recycling. Come rain or shine, if they are tired or not, they take out the bins and bring them back in. When we go away, they need to ensure it still gets done (we manage this part). Then they have earnt their allowance, so they deserve payment. In the main, they are great at it.

When I started with the pocket money exercise, my wife and I found we were getting into arrears with our children. We rarely have cash, so when pocket money day came around, they would remind us and we'd give an IOU. I knew getting into debt with our own children was not providing the right message, so I sought out a children's card called Osper. Osper offers children of eight years and above a MasterCard which is prefunded (so it has no credit card risk). We automated the payment from our Bills

Account, and they can easily pay for things in store, online or withdraw cash. They can also transfer money back to us, or to each other, using the Osper app. This system works for us.

When each child turned ten, I wanted to engage them a little more to understand, in children's terms, how the stock markets work, so we bought a share (just one share) in their favourite company. Olly at ten chose Apple, at eleven Google, and at twelve Facebook. This is not a diverse portfolio, but my intention was to explain how this stuff works for us. Now they have a healthy interest in and understanding about money, how it works and to be wise. It is a gift I hope they will never forget.

Stage one was for them to become comfortable with money, not be afraid or excited by it. At twelve, Olly started to save 10% of his income, encouraged by me. Now £2.40 pm is not much, but it's relative. If he saves 10% of his income throughout his life, it will make a massive difference to his retirement plans. When Olly and Bella each turn thirteen, it is my intention to extend their jobs to more skilled tasks so they understand the added value they can contribute.

Keeping Things on Track

I don't want you to spend all your time looking at your accounts, worrying about money. The key to financial success is automation. Set it, automate it, and leave it to work. Check in once a week to see that all the payments have gone through. Maybe have a quick view on your banking app in the morning to keep money in the forefront of your mind, but after you have been running the system for a number of months, you may not feel this is necessary.

Once a year, review all of your regular payments from your Bills Account to check which are needed going forward. In our world of automated payments, it's easier than ever to say, 'Yes, bill me on a recurring basis.' Although this works for convenience and keeps the initial costs down, the recurring payments creep up. You may have stopped going to that gym, reading that magazine, or listening to the subscription-based music, but you forgot to cancel the membership.

It's not just your Bills Account you need to look at for this. If you have previously used PayPal or similar services or credit cards, you need to check your monthly statements for payment creep.

Change your habits. If you don't, you'll remain as you are. Occasionally go without something you want, but also have some surplus in your allowance to treat yourself.

We are all human. Life gets in the way of all good plans; things will go wrong. When things do go wrong, stop, revisit your compelling vision, your values and your goals, and get right back on the programme. It's OK to screw up occasionally; it's what we do most of the time that counts. Remember, 50% of our life is spent working. We need to enjoy the process, or we'll be working for just the last 25% of our life.

Above all, get organised. Make it automatic, be happy, love life and be kind to yourself.

Summary

- Automate as many of your finances as possible
- Discuss money and what things cost with your children
- Buy your children's needs and let them buy their wants
- Join the Facebook group Facebook.com/ WarrenShuteCFP
- Set up your bank account system for bills, WAM and Emergency Reserve as a minimum
- With all your monthly payments, ask yourself, 'Do I need this payment? Do I want this payment? If so, can I buy a similar experience for less?
- Open separate savings accounts for holidays etc.
- Decide on an allowance for your children and link it to some form of effort

CHAPTER 5
Maximise Income

Once your Bills Account payments are automated and your spending money is paid into your WAM Account each week on a Wednesday, I now want you to take things up a gear. Really show you are serious about making a financial difference. Get excited about busting your debt. See how you can get rid of any debt which has been weighing you down, stopping you achieving your true potential and living life.

The faster you can clear the debt, the faster you can be free. So how do you do it?

Additional Income

If you had more money coming in, you could use all of this additional income to repay your debts. Let's imagine you could earn an extra £487 pm (that's two hours a night Monday to Friday and five hours on a Saturday based on £7.50 ph). That's going to make a big difference to how fast you are able to pay off your debts.

Ask yourself, 'How can I earn more money?' Spend some time exploring the options available to you. These could be:

- Asking for a pay rise or seeking a promotion

- Thinking how you can provide more value to the company you currently work for, so in return your boss will reward you

- Thinking how you can bring in new business or clients to the company, or increase the spending of the current clients

If you are limited in this respect, perhaps look for alternative employment. Can you get a better paid job? Start looking around to see how you can progress your career to earn more. This may involve a change of company, but consider the upside and future prospects.

If this is not an option, perhaps a second job after work and at the weekends is the solution. Working more hours will also reduce your miscellaneous spending, because you won't have time to go shopping or out with your friends.

And remember, this is not necessarily how it's going to be forever. You're making a commitment to yourself to get yourself financially well organised, to make a difference in your life, so this may involve short-term sacrifices.

> **Be committed, be brave and do what many people won't, so you can have what most people don't.**

You could also set up your own business in the evenings and at weekends. With today's technology, a one-person business can compete with the big boys and often win, due to lower cost base and more flexibility.

You may want to consider trading on eBay or other online market sites, or maybe network marketing. There are plenty of options, from skincare to utilities. Look at the business and the product range and see if it's for you.

Buying groups
One area where you can win is by using buying groups. My mother-in-law Jenny introduced Nicky and me to them, and ever since we have been avid users of buying groups to gain additional income. It surprises me how few of my clients know of them.

A buying group has agreements with various vendors. When you purchase a product via the buying group, you will receive a cashback payment. After signing up to a buying group, you log into the site, search for the retailer you want to use, click through to the retailer's site, and voila! You make your purchase. The additional step of going to the buying group site first generates a cash back which is paid into your account.

The amount of cash back and the payment terms vary quite considerably and they also change over time, so I suggest you only use buying groups where you can and don't spend too much time searching for the maximum cash back. I just appreciate receiving something.

The main two sites I use are QuidCo.com and TopCashBack.co.uk. You can sign up for both. To make life that little bit easier, you can also download a small applet (a web browser programme) which will remind you to sign into the site when you go to an approved retailer. You can register your debit card with the buying groups now, too, so when you spend face-to-face with an approved retailer, the transaction is registered and you still receive your cash back.

This is free money. Go and sign up!

Easy Fundraising

You can use another type of buying group which provides cash back, but not to you. The cash back is made to your preferred charity. Easyfundraising.org.uk works on a similar basis to the previous two companies I mentioned, providing a cash back payment to the charity you select when you sign up for the account, so it's a win-win.

Have a Good Clear Out

Some people have been consumers all their lives and have stuff lying around the place which is no longer required. Have a really good clear out. Go through your home and garage/sheds; choose one room at a time, look at everything in there, and ask yourself whether you really need it in your new life. Could someone else find it of value? You can't sell rubbish, but you may have unwanted clothes, toys or machines around the house which can be sold.

Group all the things which you feel you could sell together and go online and list them. Use sites like eBay and Facebook to list your items, spend a bit of time cleaning things up and making them look presentable, and describe them honestly. If something has a mark or a scratch, say so and let the site do the rest.

Some days are better than others to list items, and there are different periods of time you can list them for. Play around with this. There's plenty of information on the web which will help you make a success of online selling.

Every payment you receive should go straight towards your financial goals, the intention being to get yourself financially free as quickly as possible. It's not so you can enjoy more shopping, so when the payments come through, make sure you use them to:

- Top up your emergency reserve to £1,000

- Reduce your unsecured debts

- Split 40/40/20: investment/mortgage repayment/ enjoyment (I'll cover this later)

Pay the money directly into your Bills Account. Don't let it touch your WAM Account.

If you don't sell something, have a think. Would it sell at another time of year? You're unlikely to sell ski clothes in July, so maybe it's worth relisting them in winter. Nicky and I have had to list some things several times before they sold, often for more than we'd expected. Or maybe some things just won't sell at any price, or any time of year. Get a big black bin bag and throw them out.

I have suggested this to many clients over the years and they have all been able to find things to sell. They all agreed with me that this really helps put money back into their pockets.

Pricing is Paramount
Don't expect a top price for something which is of little value to you. You want rid of it and the buyer wants a bargain, so be fair and reasonable with your pricing. Having a few extra pounds in your account is better than having that old toy sitting in a cupboard, gathering dust.

When Nicky and I buy things now, we will often look ahead and think whether it is worth keeping the box. If we then come to sell it in the future, we can sell it with the original packaging. Consider this for yourself. It makes a big difference when you come to sell the items after a few years.

If you are too busy to do this, consider outsourcing the selling of the items. There are businesses out there that will sell your goods and share the profits with you.

Summary

- Try earning more income from ideas

- Sign up for the buying groups and download the browser widgets

- Have a good clear out at home and see what you can sell

- Consider keeping the packaging for new purchases in case you want to sell them on in the future

CHAPTER 6
Get Organised

Do you have debts? If so, pay attention, this will help you. Now, we need to organise your debts, when you are organised, you're in control, so the aim of this section is for you to create an organised list of your debts, knowing the interest rates and payment terms. This may take a little time, but you will likely be pleased you did it.

First step is to gather together all of your loan and credit card agreements so we can complete the following table. There is a version of this spreadsheet onWarrenShute.com/ TheMoneyPlan/Debt.

Owner	Lender	Reference	Telephone	Website Username Password	Balance (Date)	Interest Rate	Minimum Payment	Term
SECURED DEBT								
John and Jan	ABC Mortage	22544ABC	08000 987 0654	abcmortgage .co.uk *username and password	£197,432 (01/02/2017)	2.1%	£857.48 per month	23 years remaining (01/02/2040)
UNSECURED DEBT								
Jan	XYZ Financial Loan	1234XYTS	08000 1234 5667	xyzfinancial .co.uk *username and password	£8,867 (01/02/2017)	9.1%	£208.07 per month	4 years remaining (01/04/2021)
John	High Credit Card	2HIGH123	020 123 5000	2HIGH123 .co.uk *username and password	£13,500 (01/02/2017)	13.5%	£405 per month	Open

Set up a folder on your PC, or on a cloud-based service such as Google Docs or Dropbox so that you have access to it wherever you are. Being in control, being organised, is a skill that anyone can learn. Notice I said learn, not have. You will need to make different decisions to the ones you currently make to become and remain organised.

Step One

Be up to date with all your payments. If you are, great! Go to step two. If you are not, for whatever reason, we need to sort this out first.

Contact your lenders. Be open with them, explain that you have taken guidance, you are sorting your affairs out, and it's your intention to ensure this debt is repaid. But first, you will need to agree the arrears with them. Will they agree to a payment plan with you for the missed payments? Will they allow you to add the arrears to the current balance? Ensure that things are up to date and organised before you do anything else.

A payment plan is the preferred option because you will repay the arrears in a fixed period of time. If this is not an option, adding the arrears of the debt to the outstanding balance is not ideal because you are likely to pay more interest, but if it's the only way for you to become up to date, then it's necessary.

If your arrears cover more than a couple of months, take advice from a specialist company. There are many companies out there, but the one I would suggest you speak to first is Step Change (stepchange.org). Step Change, previously known as CCCS, is a charity which specialises in helping people get out of debt. If you have payment problems, arrears, or the thought of your debts is just too much, reach out and contact them for help.

Once your arrears have been sorted, then you can proceed to step two, but don't ignore this. Ensure all payments are up to date before you proceed.

Step Two

Look at the interest rates you are paying on your debts. Are these reasonable, or could they be improved by asking your current lender for a better rate, or changing the lender? There are several sites available which will help you with the interest rates of loans and credit cards. Take a look at the sites listed below which I have used in the past.

- Uswitch.com
- moneyfacts.co.uk
- moneysavingexpert.com

What you are looking to do is move your loan debt to a lower rate of interest with all other terms remaining the same, and your credit card debt to a zero interest rate balance with no or little initial fee.

If you have missed payments, the probability is that you won't be able to do this. Don't worry – skip this and focus on the initial £1,000 emergency fund section below. However, if you are able to switch your loans and credit cards, look for reasonable interest rate savings.

Where you can often save a lot of interest is with credit card balance transfers. If you have £10,000 on credit cards with an interest rate of 18.9%, that's a whopping £1,890 p.a. Look to transfer this balance to a zero rate card, which charges you no interest for a certain period of time. This period could be six months, or it could be forty-two months. There could be a transfer fee, which ranges from 0% to typically 3%. So, for up to three-and-a-half years (forty-two months), you would pay 3% (the one off initial fee), or £300. That's a £6,315 saving for a £10,000 credit card over 42 months.

There are big savings to be made here, so make sure you take a look to see if you can improve your position.

Step Three – Save £1,000

If your payments are up to date, you have a schedule of all your minimum payments and you are paying a competitive rate of interest, what I now need you to do is save £1,000.

For some of you, this will be no big deal and you'll get it sorted in a matter of months. For others, it will be the first time in your life that you have saved anything.

Remember the first time you did something? It was pretty daunting, right? It was the unknown, and you may have asked yourself, 'Can I do it?'

If you can walk, you already have a huge success story. (If you can't walk, I am sure you have succeeded in other areas.) None of us popped out at birth and ran around the room. With help, with coaching, we crawled, tumbled and stumbled, got up and fell down, but now we can walk. Why? Because we didn't give up. We tried until we were walking.

I want you to honour this self-promise: 'I will save £1,000 in the shortest time possible.' If your life, or the life of a loved one, depended on it, you'd soon find a way to save £1,000. The word 'decide' comes from the Latin 'to cut off from'. Cut off from all other possibilities, decide that you will, and each and every day take action to move closer towards the £1,000 outcome.

Deposit this money in a separate savings account or buy Premium Bonds - this is your Emergency Cash Reserve. I know the returns are low with Premium Bonds, but you are not losing much in interest by holding them. They are backed by the British government and they are out of arm's reach - this last point is important as you can't cash them in to spend at the weekend!

To buy Premium Bonds, go to NSandI.com and register. Arrange for any prize money to be reinvested to buy more Premium Bonds, with any excess being paid into your Bills Account.

At the time of writing (April 2017), the best savings rate for £1,000 was with the Bank of Scotland at 3% p.a. gross. This means that on a £1,000 deposit, you would receive 3% or £30 pa. This would fall well within the Personal Savings Allowance of £1,000 pa for basic rate tax payers or £500 p.a. for higher rate taxpayers, meaning it would be tax free.

According to the NS&I website, the odds of winning a prize on the Premium Bonds is 30,000 to 1, or 1.15%, from May 2017. So let's be clear here, it's less of a return than a savings account, but all winnings are paid tax free to everyone and you have a chance to win two £1 million prizes each month. This will provide more hope than the National Lottery. But above all, it's out of arm's reach.

Summary

Anti-debt charity Step Change says that if every household in the UK had £1,000 saved, it would reduce the number of people falling into problem debt by half a million. This is an amazing statistic. But to be clear, we're talking about £1,000 to be held in case an emergency arises. It's not to cover a night out with friends or a school trip for your children.

A survey by the Money Advice Service found that four in ten adults in the UK do not have £500 or more in savings. That's 40%. Another by ING Bank suggests 28% of UK adults have nothing at all in the bank. This won't be you. You will be financially in control, you'll have a plan and you can sleep well at night, knowing that you made a difference.

Make yourself proud. Do this, and you have taken a big step towards financial freedom.

STAGE THREE
PROTECT

CHAPTER 7
House Of Wealth Overview

Early on in my career I had a business which educated individuals on how to manage their money and invest. We ran study groups or investment clubs all across the UK, Ireland and Germany. In the late 1990s, the group developed the first version of what I am going to share with you here. I have used it since with my planning clients to illustrate where financial instruments fit in.

The House of Wealth works on the basis that we need strong foundations to build a successful financial house. Before we dive in and build our investment empire, we need to ensure we have considered the risks going forward, and if appropriate taken the necessary action to mitigate, transfer or accept the risk.

The House Of Wealth

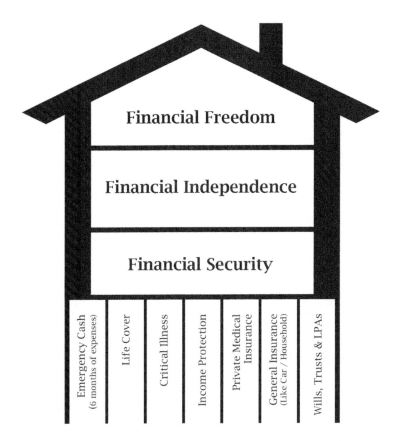

Financial Freedom

Financial Independence

Financial Security

Emergency Cash (6 months of expenses)

Life Cover

Critical Illness

Income Protection

Private Medical Insurance

General Insurance (Like Car / Household)

Wills, Trusts & LPAs

Financial Protection (The Foundations)

Everyone has the right to pursue his or her financial dreams. To turn those dreams into a reality, we must identify precisely what they are – develop our map. I have broken the financial achievements into four levels:

1. Financial Protection (the Foundations)
2. Financial Security
3. Financial Independence
4. Financial Freedom

Financial Protection (the Foundations)

Great buildings are built on strong foundations. The larger the building, the stronger the foundations.

The financial foundations supporting your House of Wealth contain various elements. Every individual will need to assess honestly what they need to include in their foundation mix. I have included a table to highlight the importance of each for different types of reader. For example:

Individuals	Couples	Retirees
Essential Could be very important Worthy of consideration Not so important	Essential Could be very important Worthy of consideration Not so important	Essential Could be very important Worthy of consideration Not so important

Emergency Cash Reserve

This is the first step on your savings ladder – the amount of money you hold on deposit in cash to cover emergencies. This should typically cover between three to twelve months of living expenses. If you have unsecured debts, hold £1,000 of cash as an Emergency Reserve, and focus on repaying your debts. For employed individuals with a secure transferable employment income, you may feel comfortable with an Emergency Reserve covering three months of expenditure. For those with their own business or a more variable income – commission only, for example – twelve months may be more appropriate. The actual amount will depend on what allows you to feel comfortable. I have some clients who would worry if they didn't hold twenty-four months reserve in cash, but this really is not necessary. These are funds you can call upon in an emergency.

If you're unsure about working it out for yourself, hold six months' worth of your monthly expenses in cash.

Individuals	Couples	Retirees
Essential	Essential	Could be very important

Life Cover

A life assurance policy would pay out a lump sum or an income (Family Income Benefit policy) if you were to die (some include terminal illness) within a fixed term (known as Term Assurance) or at any time (known as Whole of Life Assurance). If you have dependents, it's likely you will need life assurance to protect those whom you would leave behind if you died prematurely.

Typically, have sufficient life assurance to cover your mortgage and any other liabilities (car finance, credit cards and other debts you'd like to ensure were paid off if you were to die). Include your funeral expense in this allowance.

It's often better value for money if Term Assurance is arranged. This can include a renewable (not to be confused with reviewable) option. Many people prefer a Term Assurance because the premiums are less than a Whole of Life Assurance. However, you risk falling ill at the end of the term, not being able to arrange new cover and dying without any cover in place. Renewable means that you can renew the insurance term without medical evidence for a further period of time.

A couple requiring cover each will often find benefits in two individual policies, rather than a joint life policy. This is because the two individual policies have three added advantages:

1   You can each have a personalised level of cover, e.g. the main income earner may require more cover to replace lost income.

2   The individual policies can be written so the proceeds can be left into Trust rather than to the survivor directly. The main benefit of this is the speed of payout and the control of the money. If you were both to die simultaneously and the benefit were not written into Trust, it would be included within your estate and potentially be liable for Inheritance Tax.

3   The cost of a joint policy is only marginally less than the combined cost of two individual policies, but obviously on a combined claim, both policies would be payable.

There are many options with life assurance, but in the interest of simplicity, I recommend you arrange a lump sum equal to that of your debts over the longest expected term of your debt. You may choose to arrange one policy for your mortgage on a decreasing term basis (assuming you have a capital repayment mortgage) over the number of years you will have the mortgage for (it's important that this is the term remaining on the mortgage, e.g. twenty-two years, and not the number of years remaining on any special fixed rate, e.g. three years), and a second policy to cover your personal loans and credit cards on a level basis over a shorter term.

If you have dependents (children or a spouse), arrange a Family Income Benefit Term Assurance policy. This plan pays a monthly or annual amount on death (rather than a lump sum) to provide for the loss of income. The amount is paid until the end of the policy term.

There are several reasons a Family Income Benefit policy is more favourable than a lump sum to provide for loss of income on death. It's mainly because the premiums are cheaper than a lump sum term. Also, a dependent often prefers to receive a regular tax free income rather than a lump sum as there is no thinking or investment decisions to be made then. It's clean and simple.

Individuals	Couples	Retirees
Worthy of consideration	Essential	Could be very important

> **Fun is like life insurance. The older you get, the more it costs.**
> **Kin Hubbard**

Critical Illness and Serious Illness Cover

Traditionally, only Critical Illness policies were available. However, more recently, led by the insurer Vitality, a Serious Illness insurance is available.

A Critical Illness plan pays out the benefit (sum assured) in the event of a successful Critical Illness claim. A typical Critical Illness plan will cover the following conditions:

- Alzheimer's disease before age sixty – resulting in permanent symptoms

- Aorta graft surgery – for disease

- Benign brain tumour – resulting in permanent symptoms

- Blindness – permanent and irreversible

- Cancer – excluding less advanced cases

- Coma – resulting in permanent symptoms

- Coronary artery bypass grafts – with surgery to divide the breastbone

- Deafness – permanent and irreversible

- Heart attack – of specified severity

- Heart valve replacement or repair – with surgery to divide the breastbone

- HIV infection – caught in the UK from a blood transfusion, a physical assault, or at work in an eligible occupation*

- Kidney failure – requiring dialysis

- Loss of hands or feet – permanent physical severance

- Loss of speech – permanent and irreversible

- Major organ transplant

- Motor neurone disease before age sixty – resulting in permanent symptoms

- Multiple sclerosis – with persisting symptoms

- Paralysis of limbs – total and irreversible

- Parkinson's disease before age sixty – resulting in permanent symptoms

- Stroke – resulting in permanent symptoms

- Terminal illness

- Third degree burns – covering 20% of the body's surface area

- Total permanent disability – of specified severity

- Traumatic head injury – resulting in permanent symptoms

*The eligible occupations for HIV caught at work are:

- The emergency services – police, fire, ambulance

- The medical profession – including administrators, cleaners, dentists, doctors, nurses and porters

- The armed forces

Source: Association of British Insurers – *Statement of Best Practice for Critical Illness Cover* – February 2011.

More recently, Vitality came into the UK market and launched a Serious Illness insurance plan. The Vitality plan will cover a wider selection of conditions, but rather than paying out the full sum assured on the diagnosis of the illness, it will pay the claimant a predefined percentage/ proportion of the benefit (sum assured) depending on the severity of the claim. This is called a severity-based claim.

The likelihood of a successful claim is generally much higher with a severity style plan. However, you may expect a full payout because you feel your claim is critical, but the provider may only pay a proportion out if they feel the probability of a successful recovery is high.

Serious Illness policies can be more expensive than Critical Illness cover because the probability of a successful claim is far higher. You need to decide if your budget allows for this additional premium. My rule of thumb is that in an ideal world, you would have full Serious Illness cover. However, the reality is that while you have unsecured debts, prioritise the repayment of the debts. Once your unsecured debts are cleared, put some cover in place. Life assurance and income protection are essential, but serious illness can wait.

Individuals	Couples	Retirees
Could be very important	Could be very important	Worthy of consideration

Income Protection Plans

An Income Protection Plan is an insurance which will pay out if the claimant is unable to work due to an accident, long-term sickness or disability.

There are several definitions of disability. The preferable definition is Own Occupation, i.e. the policy would become payable in the event of the claimant being unable to perform his/her own occupation due to an accident or sickness. The other definitions are Any Occupation, Any Suited Occupation or Activities of Daily Living.

The tax free benefit becomes payable after a waiting period – typically three, six or twelve months, although one month policies are available, and the benefit will remain in payment until the earlier of the claimant returning to work or the end of the policy term. Often if the claimant returns to work on a reduced or pro-rata income due to the accident, then a proportion of the benefit will continue.

Individuals	Couples	Retirees
Essential	Essential	Not available

Private Medical Insurance
This provides access to UK medical consultants via a network of private hospitals. In the UK, some may feel this is an unnecessary insurance because we have the National Health Service. However, with waiting times for certain non-emergency or non-life-threatening operations being several weeks, and 'postcode lotteries' depending on what your local Primary Care Trust's budget plans will allow you to have, others will consider this as an essential insurance.

Medical policies, like all insurances, have an excess – the amount you pay before a claim is covered. Ensure this is as high as you can comfortably afford as it will keep your premiums to a minimum. I generally suggest £250, because at the time of writing, this would be the typical cost of an initial consultant's fee. Remember, private medical insurance is only used in an emergency, so the excess could be paid from your Emergency Reserve Account.

Although this is an important insurance, I suggest you arrange it after you have repaid your unsecured debts.

Individuals	Couples	Retirees
Could be very important	Could be very important	Could be very important

General Insurance

General Insurance is the insurance you are required to have to cover aspects such as your home and contents, car and travel. Find a good insurance broker or a respected online provider and ensure you have a comprehensive policy. So many people have inadequate insurance and, in the event of a claim, are unhappy with the payout. Please check your policy to ensure you are fully insured for the risks you wish to cover.

This is also an area where big savings can be made when you shop around.

Individuals	Couples	Retirees
Could be very important	Could be very important	Could be very important

Wills and Trusts

A will is a legal document in which you decide who will administer and who will benefit from your estate on your death. 'Your estate' may seem a grand term, but it is the term used to describe all of your personal possessions.

Don't leave your affairs in a mess; take pride and ensure everything is wrapped up. Sadly, a will is not just for the elderly. Anyone at any age can be struck down, so please ensure you sort your will out.

If you are struggling to know where to start with arranging a will, or you want to produce a new one, I have a website which enables you to go online at any time, day or night, and create an account. Key in the information you wish to include in your will by answering a series of simple questions – the whole process takes about fifteen minutes, and you get a bound will sent to you in the post a few days later. Go to WarrenShute.com/TheMoneyPlan/Wills.

When people have children, it's even more vital they sort out a will. If a parent dies without having made a will, a minor child will automatically be cared for by the surviving parent, assuming that parent has parental responsibility. If the child is left with no parents, then the court of protection will instruct Social Services to care for them. This means that rather than your child going to a loved one to live in familiar surroundings, they are taken into the care of Social Services until the courts can decide who should be granted guardianship. If nothing else hits you in this book, I hope this will.

Arranging a will

There are a number of different parties involved in a will. I'll list them here and give you an idea of who may fit the role, and who will not.

Role	Duties	Who to consider
Executor	An executor will administer the estate on your death. If necessary, they will close accounts, finalise payments and tidy up the administration of your estate. They will apply for probate and file any relevant forms to HMRC and pay any taxes due. Finally, they will read the will.	This person needs to be fairly organised. Administering an estate is not difficult, but it can be time-consuming. A spouse is the typical choice, then the children. However, an executor can be anyone over 18. For straightforward estate planning, I do not see the need to appoint a professional executor, mainly because of the costs involved. Your chosen executor can always seek legal guidance from a lawyer if this is required to help them do the job.

Role	Duties	Who to consider
Guardian	A guardian will be the person you entrust to care for your children. The children become the responsibility of the guardian until they are of an age they can care for themselves.	I would suggest you first look at people whom your children know. If your children have lost both of their parents, the last thing they need is more uncertainty. When choosing a guardian, minimise change. This will not always be possible with families living further apart in a modern world, but the more continuity you can keep in your children's lives, the more stable their future will be. Maintaining the same location for schooling and friends will go towards supporting this. Finally, choose an individual, rather than a couple. You can always include reserve guardians if the first selected guardian is unable or unwilling to take on the role. By avoiding naming a couple as guardians, you have certainty of your guardian if their relationship breaks down in the future.

Role	Duties	Who to consider
Trustee	A trustee is a person or a company you entrust to make the decisions on your behalf, in this case, because you are deceased. For example, you leave £100,000 in your will to your children. Your children are minors, say three and five years old. The trustees will look after the £100,000 not for their own benefit, but for the benefit of your children. It's a fiduciary responsibility. The trustees will do whatever is necessary to care for the trust assets. In the example above, the £100,000 cash will be bound legally by the Trustee Act. Trustees would need to open bank accounts and invest the funds as necessary. The settlor is the person to set up the trust, so in the case of a trust in a will (a will trust), this is the deceased. So, the deceased (settlor) should write a letter of wishes which guides the trustees. This is not binding, but helps the trustees when they are making decisions for the benefit of the beneficiaries (person/people who are entitled to benefit from the trust assets).	When selecting trustees, you always need at least two, or a company, known as a corporate trustee. The legal profession may suggest its services, which is fine if your affairs are more complex. However, for the everyday mum and dad situation in the UK, selecting a sensible friend or relative will work fine. There is nothing stopping your selected trustees from taking legal and accounting advice from a professional when running the trust.

Role	Duties	Who to consider
Beneficiary	The beneficiaries are the people or person who will benefit from the Will.	The beneficiaries can be main beneficiaries and catastrophe beneficiaries. A main beneficiary is who you intend to inherit. This may be an individual, charity, political party, or in some cases, a company. A catastrophe beneficiary is often a fallback or reserve, in case a catastrophe were to occur and the main beneficiaries were deceased at the time of your death. Catastrophe beneficiaries can include a charity. Leaving an inheritance to a charity has benefits. Any money left to a charity is inheritance tax free, and if you leave at least 10% of your net estate to a charity, it will reduce your inheritance tax rate from 40% to 36%. The payments made to beneficiaries from a will come in the following three forms: **Specific bequests/ gifts** – an item you leave to a beneficiary. e.g. my jewellery to my daughter. **Legacies** – an amount of money you leave to a beneficiary. e.g. £1,000 to each of my nephews. **Residue** – everything else which remains in the estate after gifts and legacies. e.g. my residue to my spouse.

Individuals	Couples	Retirees
Essential	Essential	Essential

Lasting Power of Attorney (LPA)

We all need a power of attorney if we are over eighteen. It enables someone we trust to completely manage our money and property, and decide on our welfare if we lose mental capacity. That is, if we can't make decisions for ourselves.

There are two types of LPA: Property and Financial Affairs and Health and Welfare. The Financial LPA can be used as soon as it has been registered with the Office of the Public Guardian, unless you have specified otherwise. However, the Health and Welfare LPA can only be used once it has been registered and you are unable to make a decision for yourself because you have lost mental capacity.

The people who you trust to make decisions on your behalf, when you are unable, are called your attorneys, and they're usually friends or family members.

When to Think About Setting Up a Power of Attorney

You must have mental capacity to make your own decisions when you set up a Power of Attorney. It's a good idea to get it set up well before you need it; it's much harder and more expensive for someone to help you with your money and property if you've already lost mental capacity. And if you get it set up now, it's there if something happens to you suddenly. Go to WarrenShute.com/TheMoneyPlan/LPA to arrange one now.

It takes several weeks to register a Lasting Power of Attorney – yet another reason to get it set up early. If you lose mental capacity during those weeks, your attorney would not be able to act for you in the meantime.

Your attorney should be someone you really trust. For most people, that's their husband, wife, partner, another family member or a close friend. Your attorney could also be a professional, for example your solicitor, but that usually costs money, and for people whose affairs are straightforward, it's not usually necessary.

You might want to choose more than one attorney. If you do, you can say whether they need to make decisions jointly (a good idea if you want two opinions on your finances) or whether each can decide things without the other (good for spreading the load).

Consider logistics. If your attorneys live in New Zealand, it may take some time to get things sorted. Also choose at least one replacement attorney who will take over if your attorney dies or can no longer act for you. If you are older and the people you choose are all the same age as you, they may not end up being the best people to act for you if and when you need their help.

Types of Lasting Power of Attorney

The big differences between the types of power of attorney are the decisions they cover. The options available depend on where you live.

England and Wales. There are two types of Lasting Power of Attorney. A Property and Financial Affairs Lasting Power of Attorney lets someone manage all your financial affairs – for example, running your bank and savings accounts, managing your tax affairs, and buying and selling investments (including pensions in drawdown) and property. A Health and Welfare Lasting Power of Attorney lets someone make decisions about your health, care and welfare – for example, what medical treatment you receive and whether you move into a care home.

You can set up one or both. I suggest you set up both now.

Scotland. There are two types of Lasting Power of Attorney: a Continuing Power of Attorney lets someone manage all your financial affairs. A Welfare Power of Attorney lets someone make decisions about your care and welfare.

Northern Ireland. There is only one type of power of attorney, an Enduring Power of Attorney. It lets someone manage all your financial affairs, similar to the English Property and Financial Affairs Lasting Power of Attorney. There isn't a power of attorney that lets someone make decisions about your health and wellbeing.

Setting up a Power of Attorney

You can either arrange these yourself by using the government website, or use my step by step process atWarrenShute.com/TheMoneyPlan/LPA.

Individuals	Couples	Retirees
Essential	Essential	Essential

Financial Security

Once you have covered the financial foundations, you are ready to move on to the financial security level.

You have achieved financial security when:

- You have repaid all unsecured debts, leaving you with only secured debts such as a mortgage
- You have saved three to twelve months of emergency fund

> " **Time is key to building your
> financial security.** "
>
> Suze Orman

Financial Independence

Financial independence moves you into the investment area. You have achieved financial independence when, through various investments, you have accumulated a critical mass of capital which, when invested in a secure environment at 4% return, provides you with enough income to meet your 'basic' living needs forever without you having to work again. This could be an income generated from a business or property.

I define your basic living needs as:

- Monthly mortgage payments on your home until the mortgage is repaid
- Family food needs each month
- Utilities such as gas/oil, electric, council tax, telephone, mobile, broadband and property insurance
- Travel costs such as car payments, servicing, road tax and fuel
- Taxes

In summary, your financial independence reflects your basic current lifestyle.

Financial Freedom

Once financial independence is achieved, the next stage for you to aim towards is financial freedom. You have achieved financial freedom when, through various investments, you have accumulated a critical mass of capital which, when invested in a secure environment at 4% return, provides you with enough income to meet your desired living needs forever, without you having to work again.

I define desired living needs as the following:

- Monthly mortgage payments on your home until the mortgage is repaid.
- Family food needs each month
- Utilities such as gas/oil, electric, council tax, telephone, mobile, broadband and property insurance
- Travel costs such as your car payments, servicing, road tax and fuel
- Taxes
- WAM spending
- Holidays and recreation – cinema, theatre, health club, etc.

In summary, your financial freedom reflects your 'reasonable' current lifestyle.

> **Financial freedom is available to those who learn about it and work for it.**
> Robert Kiyosaki

Summary

- Make sure you have adequate cover in place for all eventualities
- Arrange a will
- Arrange both power of attorneys
- Review the financial foundations to see what is important to you
- Know your financial independence number and your financial freedom number

A summary of your foundation needs

Lump Sum/Income	Increasing/Level/Decreasing	Amount	Term
Emergency Reserve (now)			
Minimum of £1,000 while you hold unsecured debts, rising to three to twelve months outgoings once cleared.			

Life Assurance (now)			
Lump sum to cover mortgage	Decreasing Term Assurance	Amount of your current mortgage balance	For the term of your mortgage (not the interest rate)
Lump sum to cover unsecured debts	Level Term Assurance	Amount to cover all other debts	For the term of your longest debt
Insurance to replace your income on death	Family Income Benefit Increasing By Rpi	Your net take home income less mortgage and debt repayment	Until your dependents are twenty-one

Serious Illness/Critical Illness Cover (once unsecured debts are repaid)			
Serious Illness or Critical Illness (if affordable)	Level Term Assurance increasing by RPI	Look at £100,000 if this is affordable	Terms past normal retirement become expensive, so preferably to state retirement age

Lump Sum/Income	Increasing/Level/ Decreasing	Amount	Term
Income Protection (now)			
Insurance to replace your income on disability	Income Protection increasing by RPI	The maximum you can arrange, usually 50–70% of income	To your state retirement age (sixty-six to sixty-eight years old). A deferred/ waiting period of three months (this will be covered by your emergency reserve)

Private Medical Insurance (once unsecured debts are repaid)			
Medical Insurance	Comprehensive Cover	Full Inpatient Cover Full Outpatient Cover	Excess of £250 per year

General Insurance (now)			
Home and Contents, Car Insurance, Travel Insurance	Comprehensive Cover	Check your Buildings and Contents valuations	Higher excess will reduce your premiums

Wills, Trust and Lasting Powers of Attorneys (now)
Ensure these are arranged promptly

STAGE FOUR
DEBT

CHAPTER 8
Clearing The Debt Burden

The Snowball

Do you have unsecured debt? Are you ready to clear that debt?

Once you have listed all your debts, sold any unwanted items and maximised your income, this is what you need to do next. We are going to use a proven system which will maximise each payment to accelerate the repayment of your debts while motivating you to remain on the programme.

Take the list of your debts and put them in order of balance size, with the smallest balance first. Let's call the smallest Debt Number 1, the second smallest Number 2, and so on. Now ensure you continue to make the minimum payment on each of your credit agreements automatically each month. These payments should be set up from your Bills Account by direct debit or maybe standing order.

But if you only pay the minimum payment, you'll be repaying these from your grave. Our plan is to clear the debt burden in the fastest way possible while continuing to have a life.

By now, hopefully you are organised. You know what money is coming in and it's been maximised, what's going out each month, you've cut all unwanted waste, and what you owe is organised in a format that gives you all the information you need. So let's take the next step to repay the debt you have built up.

> **There are no shortcuts when it comes to getting out of debt.**
> **Dave Ramsey**

The snowball is the surplus funds which you have available each month. It can be calculated as follows:

Total Income from all sources – Bills Account payments*
= Surplus or Snowball.

*Your Bills Account payments include your WAM Account payments

Your snowball should be at least 12.5% of your gross (before tax) monthly income. This 12.5% represents the first hour of your working day. This small commitment will make a significant difference to your financial future.

I want you to take your snowball, in addition to any other spare cash you have each month (bear in mind you only spend your WAM and your bills are taken care of), and repay the balance onto debt number 1 on your list. Repeat this process each month until debt number 1 is repaid. Then, close the account. You don't need it any more. When you're losing weight, you don't leave your weakness around the house – you won't find a pizza in my fridge when I am in training. Debt is just the same.

Once Debt Number 1 is repaid, take the two payments you were making to that debt (the minimum payment plus the snowball) and add this to the repayments of Debt Number 2. This larger overpayment is your new snowball, hence the name. As momentum builds, the overpayment keeps growing.

You keep paying Debt Number 2's minimum payment in addition to the new larger snowball and all your other spare cash until this is repaid, then close this account too. Once Debt Number 2 is repaid, take the minimum payment you were making to Debt Number 2 and the snowball and add this to the repayments on Debt Number 3, and so on.

This will not only accelerate the repayment of your debts, but will also help significantly with your passion, enthusiasm and commitment to repaying these debts as fast as you can. Remember, we are looking for lifetime habits, longevity. You would get a better 'bang for your buck' by repaying your highest interest rate debt first, but the time you take to repay this debt may erode your motivation, and motivation, passion and enthusiasm are the keys to this process. So stick to the smallest balance first, get a quick win and build momentum.

The table opposite shows how the snowball may work in an example.

You can download a snowball repayment spreadsheet from the website WarrenShute.com/TheMoneyPlan/Snowball to help you keep track and forecast when your debts will be repaid.

Lender	Balance	Interest	Minimum payment	Snowball for 6 months	Snowball for 8 months	Snowball for 10 months
XYZ Financial Debt 2	£9,867 (01/02/2017)	9.1%	£296.01 per month		£1,181.50 (£1,000 + £181.50)	
ABC Card Debt 3	£15,549 (01/02/2017)	4.1%	£446.47 per month			£1,477.51 (£1,000 + £181.50 + £296.01)
Fast Card Debt 1	£6,050 (01/02/2017)	7.5%	£181.50 per month	£1,000		

Save your Emergency Fund

If you hold unsecured debt, before you start increasing your Emergency Reserve Fund, you need to get that repaid. Follow the snowball system to accelerate the debt repayment. Once you are unsecured debt-free, you can take a deep breath, stretch your arms out in front of you, wrap them around your body and give yourself a big hug.

> **Before you start increasing your Emergency Reserve fund, follow the snowball steps to repay all unsecured debt.**

You have just completed what many people will never do – you have made sacrifices for a better life. Take a moment to savour this experience; take in what you have really accomplished.

Now you should have £1,000 in Premium Bonds, or another savings account, which has been there to support you so far during your journey. Did you need to use it? Or was it just a teacher for you? I say a 'teacher' because if you wanted to use it at times for the wrong reasons, whether you did or didn't, it was there to teach you that you can do this.

We are now going to take you to another level.

When you started this journey, you may not have appreciated you would arrive at this day. You may not have believed in yourself, but you believed in me and the process. I need you to go to that belief again and trust me.

You should have £1,000 in Premium Bonds or savings. But, if you had a serious problem, the £1,000 wouldn't last long and you'd end up using credit cards or loans again to make ends meet. We need to prevent that.

Financial planners from all walks of life will tell you that you need three to twelve months of expenditure as an Emergency Fund Reserve. But three months and twelve months is a massive variance, so which one do you need?

How much you need in an Emergency Fund will depend on your personal employment position and expenditure. If you are an employee, easily employable and/or have no dependents, then three months will probably work well for you. If you're self-employed with a family and have an 'earn to burn' income pattern (what I mean by that is you earn it today and spend it tomorrow), then lean towards twelve months.

There's no right or wrong answer; I can just say to you that you definitely need at least three months. You will know – the ideal amount is whatever makes you feel safe and allows you to sleep well at night.

If you have never held cash before, six months' worth to start with will be brilliant.

Whatever your choice, add up all your payments from your Bills Account (which includes your WAM) and multiply this figure by the amount of months' expenditure you want to cover. Hold this money where the £1,000 sits right now; there's no need to open another account.

You can go to WarrenShute.com/TheMoneyPlan/ Expenditure and download a spreadsheet which will help you do this.

Your full Emergency Fund may take you some weeks to accumulate, but I want you to go at it with the same passion, excitement and commitment you had for the debt repayment. Find innovative and exciting ways to earn more money and sell unwanted items. Maybe you could sell your friends' unwanted items too. Do it now and get your Emergency Fund saved. Take every penny you were using for your snowball and redirect it to your Emergency Reserve account. Make it automatic.

Once you have completed this, take another moment to appreciate what you have just accomplished – all unsecured debt repaid and a fully funded Emergency Reserve. You have achieved financial mastery – security level.

Summary

- Repay the smallest debt first for a dopamine boost
- Calculate your snowball
- Set the snowball payment up to be automatic
- Before you start increasing your Emergency Reserve Fund, follow the snowball steps to repay all unsecured debt
- Consider how secure your income is. How transferable are your skills?
- Calculate your Emergency Reserve amount. If you're unsure, choose six months
- When your unsecured debts are repaid, set your snowball payment to deposit into your Emergency Reserve Account (Premium Bonds or savings account)

CHAPTER 9
40/40/20

We now set off to work towards Financial Mastery –
Independence and Freedom Level.

As we begin this stage of your journey, you must have
your financial banking in order. You need the insurance in
place to protect you and your family, you will have repaid
all your unsecured debt and will only have your mortgage
remaining, and will have a fully funded Emergency Reserve.

You now may want to consider Critical/Serious Illness
cover and private medical insurance as you grow your

House of Wealth. These can be valuable insurances to have, but be careful. You want to keep the momentum going, so avoid the complacency of the comfort zone.

For example, say you start an eating programme with the goal of losing 14 pounds. After six weeks, you're 10 pounds down and looking good. You've not hit your goal, but you're happy with the benefits of that weight loss – more energy, better health, greater life focus, social fun. So you stop doing the actions that got you to where you are today and slip back into your old habits – the ones which, because you've been doing them for so many years, are easier, stronger and, at present, still habitual. You have moved your focus away from fitness and fat loss, and slowly the weight starts creeping back on.

We are creatures of habit. It's our habits that make us and our habits that break us.

This is the comfort zone – the most dangerous place for anyone to be. We need a driving, compelling future, and we must programme our brain (our amazing control panel) daily to make new habits which support us. Make growth your friend; make progress enjoyable. I need you to remember your why – why you really want this. Keep reading your Compelling Vision and goals each night and every morning to programme yourself for financial success.

So, with that in mind, let's not waste any more time, let's get started.

If you interviewed 100 financial experts, you would get a wide range of responses. From my experience, half would tell you to repay your debts before investing, and the other half would suggest you invested first, if the interest rates were reasonable.

When you pay your monthly debt payments – your loans, credit card bills, mortgage – these are paid typically from your after tax income. So when you look at the true cost of the interest you are paying, gross the interest up by your rate of income tax. For example, if you are paying 5% interest on your debt and you are a 20% income tax payer (this means you earn up to approximately £45,000 p.a.), the true cost of the interest is 6.25% (5%/(100%–20%)). Depending on your interest rates, this could be significant.

If you were to repay your debt, you'd have a guaranteed return on your investment – a saving of the gross interest. Few investments offer such guaranteed returns. This is partly why we focus on repaying unsecured debts first as these often have the highest interest rates and highest monthly payments. Although we can arrange 0% credit card transfers, we don't know how long they will remain available and the minimum payments make them expensive for our cash flow.

Some financial experts may argue that yes, the above is true, but the long-term total return of the stock market is over 11% (FTSE All Share total return over the last thirty-five years). That is far higher than your interest costs, so why don't you just leave your borrowing in place and view the interest cost as a charge against the 11% growth you'll get over the years? The power of compound growth has a miracle effect on your wealth, and when you start making money on your money, the snowball effect works in your favour with an escalating amount of capital.

The one thing these experts often leave out is the positive effect of the pride and confidence that builds when you see your investments growing. The psychological boost of being an investor and becoming wealthy is massive, especially if you have never had money invested before. The way I see it is that both investing and paying off your debts work. So, I want you to take both courses of action simultaneously. Take 40% of your snowball payment and add it to your mortgage repayment as an overpayment, take another 40% and add it to your Investment Fund. Then take the remaining 20% and add it to your Fun Account.

The Fun Account is a separate bank account which you can spend on whatever you wish (but don't take out any debt). You may want to travel, you may want to learn a new instrument or take up a hobby. This account is for you to enjoy, so live your life and reward yourself for the sacrifices and effort you have put in.

I have recommended a 40/40/20 split because this is a lifestyle financial plan. I want you to stick to this programme. It's not about saving up as much as you can for a future date; it's about being in control – financial mastery.

Repaying the debt will increase your financial security and provide you with better cash flow when the monthly payments end. Investing will change your mindset from a novice to a master, give you confidence and provide you with more options. Your Fun Account will be like your Holiday Account (perhaps even the same account) where you make an automatic payment from your Bills Account. It's your financial version of a cheat meal.

If you can't overpay on your mortgage due to redemption penalties, I still want you to allocate the overpayment of the snowball, but rather than applying it to repaying the mortgage account, deposit the funds into a savings account or Premium Bonds. Do this each month automatically, then once your redemption penalties have ended, before you change your rate, make a single capital repayment from this account to your mortgage to reduce the balance. This is not perfect, but it's your best option.

Once your mortgage debt is repaid and you are completely debt free, you can change the allocation, depending on how on track you are for financial freedom. If you are on track, change the allocation to 60% towards investment and 40% towards fun. However, if you're a late starter, or you need a little more of a boost in your retirement savings, take the 40% from your mortgage overpayment and add it straight into your Investment Account. You'll need to make an assessment at this stage of your financial development.

Of course, I understand that not everyone owns their own home, and if you come into this category, you actually have something of a head start. As soon as your unsecured debts are paid off, you will be debt free and can move straight to the 60/40% allocation split: 60% towards investment and 40% for fun. Rent payments, being ongoing payments, will need to be covered by your Bills Account.

The next two chapters will discuss your mortgage snowball and your investment snowball, but for now, congratulations! You're on your way to financial mastery.

To summarise, your snowball is the amount of money remaning after all Bills Account payments (which includes your weekly WAM) are made. You need to ensure this is at least 12.5% of your gross income.

Allocation of snowball

The allocation of your snowball payment while paying a mortgage is:

- 40% Investment Bucket
- 40% Mortgage Overpayment Bucket
- 20% Fun Bucket

Once your mortgage has been repaid, you need to assess where you are financially and if you feel you are on track for your retirement.

Snowball allocation – on track

I recommend for most of you reallocating your snowball payment from the 40/40/20 to:

- 60% Investment Bucket
- 40% Fun Bucket

Snowball allocation – catch-up

If you are a late starter and need to play catch up, I recommend you give the full allocation of the debt payment to investment:

- 80% Investment Bucket
- 20% Fun Bucket

Allocation of your snowball savings for a house deposit
Take a balanced approach to buying your first home. With your snowball, I want you to allocate no more than 60% to your deposit savings, ensuring you still invest 20% and have 20% for fun bucket. You may decide to sacrifice the fun bucket allocation for a while, but remember life is for living. I don't want you to forgo your retirement savings – this is important, and you must save at least 12.5% of your income. Remember, make your first hour count.

- 20% Investment Bucket
- 60% Mortgage Deposit Savings Bucket
- 20% Fun Bucket

Summary

- Repaying your debts provides certainty
- Investing can build your financial confidence
- Calculate your 40/40/20 split of your snowball
- Make your 40/40/20 snowball split automatic

CHAPTER 10
Mortgage Snowball

The first step in repaying your mortgage debt as fast as possible is to ensure you are paying the lowest level of interest you reasonably can.

The interest that the mortgage lender charges you is based on a couple of factors: general economic conditions of the UK and your personal financial profile. Interest rates move up and down over economic cycles. It just so happens at the time of writing this book in April 2017 that interest rates in the UK are the lowest I have ever seen in my twenty-plus years as a financial planner.

Interest rates often increase when the economic cycle increases, i.e. the economy does well. This is because when spending increases, the cost of goods increases, and this increase is measured by inflation. It's the Bank of England's responsibility to ensure inflation (the measure of the increase in the cost of goods) is kept under control. One way in which it can slow spending and therefore slow inflation is by increasing interest rates – how much our borrowing costs us. If we have less money left after paying our borrowing because of the higher rate of interest, we will spend less.

If inflation were allowed to increase indefinitely, without being kept under control, the cost of goods would become excessively expensive, and ultimately the pound would become worthless as an international currency. The UK monetary policy is very strict and respected internationally, and thus Sterling is a strong currency.

Inflation is taxation without legislation.
Milton Friedman

If interest rates are used to control inflation, when inflation starts to pick up, one might expect interest rates to pick up too. At the time of writing, the United States increased interest rates on 14 December 2016 from 0.5% to 0.75% and again on 15 March 2017 from 0.75% to 1%. The UK actually reduced rates on 4 August 2016 from 0.5% to 0.25%. However, inflation is increasing and international rates are slowing looking to rise, so we may see rates rise in the UK going forward.

When you look at the rates available to you in the mortgage market, decide if you will choose a tracker rate, which is a variable interest rate and often tracks either the Bank of England Base rate (preferred option) or your lender's variable rate (least preferred option), or a fixed rate, which means you will pay that rate of interest for a fixed period of time. The term of the fixed rate can be anything from twelve months to ten years, but they are most often fixed for a two- to five-year period.

It would be wrong for me to tell you to choose a tracker or a fixed interest rate as you need to know what is available to you at the time of selecting and your own plans, e.g. moving house, etc., but while rates are so low, take advantage of this. Consider fixing your payment, if you can, for as long as reasonable.

You also need to look at the fees associated with the mortgage. These can make a massive difference to whether you save money overall or not. Cheaper is not always better; it may depend on your mortgage size as many fees are fixed price and therefore reflect a lower percentage on larger mortgages. Look at the overall fees (these include interest rates) and make a call.

All of the costs of a mortgage are included in the Key Facts Illustration or European Standard Information Sheet (ESIS). Take time to read these and compare your options. moneyadviceservice.org.uk/en/articles/keyfacts-documents-explaining-your-mortgage

Some of the criteria I look for in a mortgage are:

No Extended Tie-in
The special rate of interest which a lender offers you, e.g. the tracker rate for two years or the five year fixed rate, often (not always) has a tie-in or commitment to that lender for that period of time. This is known as the redemption penalty period. If you are arranging a five year fixed rate, it would be fairly common for you to be committed to your lender for five years, so if you leave them, i.e. repay your mortgage, you also need to repay the redemption penalties. These are often a percentage of the mortgage and can run into many thousands of pounds.

Some mortgage lenders extend these penalties after the special rate ends and you're then on their standard variable rate. You don't know what this will be in the future. If interest rates with your lender are not competitive when your rate expires and you have extended tie-ins, you may not be able to afford to move, but you also may not be able to afford the payments.

Don't, under any circumstances, accept extended redemption penalties. It's too risky.

Ability to Overpay

You're after financial freedom, which means repaying all debt as soon as possible. Although you may arrange your mortgage over a fifteen to forty-year term to ensure that the contractual minimum payments are affordable, you must have the ability to overpay without penalty.

How much lenders allow you to overpay will vary from lender to lender, and you will need to look at this when considering the mortgage. Basically, the higher the free overpayment amount, the better, but there's no need to forgo a great mortgage rate with a good overpayment level for a higher rate with a significant overpayment allowance. You will be overpaying 40% of your snowball, so this will give you a good idea of the overpayment amount you will make each month.

Portable Mortgage

You may plan to remain in your home indefinitely, you may not want to move to a larger, or smaller, place, but life gets in the way of our well-intentioned plans. Work may relocate, a family illness may necessitate a move, or relationships don't always work out as planned.

A Portable Mortgage is one which you can move across to a new property, assuming the new property meets the lender's criteria. For example, if you live in Exeter and you need to move to Leicester, as long as the property you move to is of similar value (same or higher) to your current one and you meet the lender's other criteria, you simply move the current mortgage to the new property and do not pay any redemption penalties (apart from the lender's administration fees).

Daily Rest or Interest

Interest can be calculated on your mortgage balance either daily, monthly or annually. The majority of lenders use the more attractive daily interest, but a few lenders out there still calculate it annually. Then when you overpay on your mortgage, you are not getting the immediate benefit of this overpayment. It pays to check.

Arrangement Fees Added to the Advance

Arrangement Fees are the fees that lenders charge you to

arrange a mortgage. They are not a broker's or mortgage adviser's fee. If you pay this upfront and your application fails for some reason, very often it is not refundable. If you ask for the fee to be added to the mortgage on completion and your application fails, most often you are not liable for the fee.

Once your mortgage starts, I recommend your first payment is to repay the arrangement fee you added. If you do not repay this immediately, you will be charged interest on it, and over the term of the mortgage, your few hundred pounds arrangement fee may well turn into a few thousand.

There are other features to mortgages, but I would prefer you avoid these for now:

Offset or Current Account Mortgages
These are great mortgage options. However, that's what they are: options. If the rate of interest is not competitive, and often it is not, then don't use them. You want to be paying the lowest rates of interest possible, so most of your payment goes against the capital outstanding.

An Offset Mortgage offsets the mortgage balance against any savings you have with the lender. For example, let's say you have £50,000 in savings – this could be your emergency fund – and you have a £225,000 mortgage balance. The mortgage lender would offset the £50,000 savings against your mortgage balance of £225,000 and charge you interest on the difference of £175,000, while not paying you interest on the £50,000. This is a great interest saver if you are committed and disciplined, but please don't fool yourself if you're not.

Current Account Mortgages are similar. A Current Account Mortgage is basically a large overdraft where your current account is operated via your mortgage. Your income is paid into the mortgage account and has an immediate repayment effect, and the mortgage balance reduces, thus saving you interest. Then all your bills are taken out of the mortgage and the account increases. The period from pay going in and bills coming out has saved you interest.

In theory, this is great, but you need to be strong and disciplined with money to make this work as well in practice as it does on paper.

If you like the flexible mortgage options, I'd prefer you to go for the offset route, keeping savings and your mortgage effectively in separate accounts, rather than a current account mortgage.

Currency Mortgages
This is where you take a Euro or Dollar mortgage out and hope that in the fullness of time, the currency change

between Sterling and the Euro or Dollar goes in your favour. All I am going to say is don't do it. Do. Not. Do. It.

Get the best mortgage rate with the flexibility of the options mentioned above and you will be in a great position. In the current economic climate, I'd suggest looking closely at longer term fixed rates, but if these are expensive, consider shorter term fixed or tracker rates, preferably tracking the Bank of England (BoE) and not the lender bank base rate (BBR). And remember, under no circumstances accept extended tie-ins.

Now we have covered mortgages, we need to turn to using your snowball payment. I want you to use 40% of your snowball to overpay your mortgage. You will then see the benefit of the daily interest rate charge. Once that payment hits the mortgage account, it will reduce your interest cost and repay your mortgage sooner. Set up a standing order from your Bills Account directly to your Mortgage Account (remember to use your account number as a reference) to make the snowball overpayment.

Your monthly mortgage payment comprises of capital and interest. If your snowball payment equals the capital portion of your monthly payment (you will be able to see what this is from your Key Facts illustration) and you were to overpay this amount each month, based on a £225,000 mortgage at 2.5% interest over twenty-five years, you would reduce the term to fourteen-and-a-half years, a reduction of over ten years or 40% of the term. This would save you almost £35,000 in interest. You are effectively paying the capital before the interest can be charged on it, but what I want you to do is to overpay the full 40% of your snowball. This may be in excess of the capital portion, so you will have a greater repayment effect.

The following chart shows a light grey and a dark grey line. The light grey line represents a £225,000 mortgage over twenty-five years with no overpayments. The dark grey line shows the effect of the mortgage balance repayment accelerating with the capital overpayment each month.

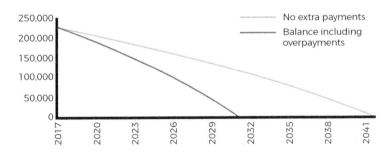

When you come into additional money from household sales, overtime/bonus or wherever, pay 40% of this into the mortgage. Another 40% will be allocated to investment and the remaining 20% to your Fun Account.

Get determined, be persistent and get joy from accelerating your mortgage debt payments.

Summary

- You can save thousands by reducing your interest rate
- You will save thousands by accelerating your over-payment
- Get the best mortgage rate you can
- Set your snowball overpayment to be automatic

STAGE FIVE
INVEST

CHAPTER 11
Investment Success

When we invest, we are putting our hard-earned capital at risk to grow in value. Because our money will fluctuate in value, we need to listen to the people who have studied this for a living.

> **Risk comes from not knowing what you are doing.**
> **Warren Buffett**

I will walk you step by step through how to invest intelligently.

First of all, when you're investing there are three main considerations:

- Term – how long will you invest for until you need access to your capital?
- Investment risk – how much risk will you accept with your capital? When I refer to risk, I mean how much it can fluctuate (fall and rise) in value
- Wrapper – which wrapper or account will you hold your investments in, e.g. a Pension, ISA or General Account?

The clearer we can be with our decisions, the better our investment experience is likely to be.

The term of the investment is how long we plan to have our investment capital committed. We need to know when we plan to access the capital, or receive the income from the capital invested, before we start investing. We don't need to be specific with a date, but we need to know approximately how many years this will be. The longer the time frame, the more enjoyable our experience is likely to be. I cover this in more detail later.

We also need to know the level of risk we are willing to accept with our capital. I typically define this as, 'how much could the value of your investment fall before you would begin to feel uncomfortable?'

These two decisions are related. The risk we accept with our portfolio or investment is often linked to the amount of equity in our portfolio. The more equity or stock market exposure, the higher the risk or 'ups and downs' the portfolio will experience.

So how much risk should you accept? An old rule of thumb is for you to hold a percentage of your capital equalling 100 minus your age in equities, so a forty-year-old would have 100 – 40 or 60% of their capital in equities. Now, I believe this is a good rule of thumb. When you are younger, it's good to have a higher equity allocation, but when you are in your sixties, holding 40% equities seems quite sensible if you intend to remain invested. However, the only caveat I will include is you must be comfortable with the potential falls that the portfolio you choose can experience.

What I mean by this is that a portfolio of 100% equity will (not may) fall significantly more than a portfolio with only 20% equity. Your investment provider should be able to share with you the maximum historical loss of the portfolio, and you want this information to stretch back at least ten years, preferably more.

As a rough guide, you can expect a portfolio to fall by about 50% of the equity allocation (this may be extreme but a good guide). So, for example, a 100% equity portfolio is likely to experience 50% falls in its value before recovering, and a 60% equity portfolio will experience approximately 30% falls before recovering. But I don't know specifically what you'll be investing in, so there's no way I can be accurate on a broad subject like this. However, if you want more details, go to Lexo.co.uk where portfolios, risks and returns are all online to view.

> **The most important investment you can make is in yourself.**
> **Warren Buffett**

So in summary, choose a portfolio which will allow you to sleep well at night and provide you with the best potential for capital growth. If you are unsure what portfolio to buy, an Index Lifestyle Fund is a good solution. This is a managed portfolio which uses Index Funds (Tracker Funds which are low cost), and the risk of the portfolio reduces over time.

Now, I want to look at the third decision which you need to make: which wrapper or account type is appropriate.

There are three main investment wrappers available:

- General Investment Accounts or GIAs
- Stocks and Shares Individual Savings Accounts or ISAs
- Personal Pension Plans or PPPs

Each has benefits and drawbacks. The key is to match the benefits of the wrapper to what's important to you.

If you want details around each of these, there is a download available on WarrenShute.com/TheMoneyPlan/Wrapper

Pensions first

Your first priority for your investment contributions is to maximise your pension wrapper annual allowance. Pensions are funded from before tax money. When you pay into a pension personally, you do so with after tax money, then the pension provider will reclaim the basic rate of income tax back for you and add this to your contribution.

As if this wasn't good enough, if you pay a higher rate of income tax than the basic rate, you can reclaim the extra difference either by completing a self-assessment tax return or by sending HMRC a letter. I have posted a letter template at WarrenShute.com/TheMoneyPlan/HMRC_ Letter.

If your employer or company pays the pension payments on your behalf, you are likely to pay these before income tax is deducted, so it's an even better position to be in. But check with your employer how your pension scheme has been set up to be sure.

This makes pension the number one choice when you're starting your retirement savings. The only exception is if you have slightly more complex pension affairs and you have applied for a form of pension fund protection, in which case seek professional advice first. But for the majority, pensions work.

How much should you start to invest? From your initial snowball, I want you to allocate 40% to pensions and your investments. Remember, once this money is funded into a pension, it is tied up until you're fifty-five. See this as an advantage. You are putting money from your bank account into a tax-free wrapper, protected from temptation and creditors should anything go wrong for you financially.

It's very likely your employer will have offered you a Workplace Pension. If so, the first step is for you to ensure you are fully funding this. Some generous employers will match whatever you contribute to the pension scheme, up to a limit. For example, you could be funding 2% at present, and your employer is matching this. However, if they will match up to 5% of whatever you pay in, this should be your next step. Fund 5% to obtain the matched benefit.

This is effectively greater than a 100% return on your contribution because of the tax relief.

Pensions are important, mainly for the tax relief you receive on the contributions. For every £100 you contribute personally, HMRC will add £25 to this so £125 will be invested. That's a 25% return on your investment from day one. If you pay higher rate (40%) or additional rate (45%) income tax, it makes a pension even more attractive.

Let me show you how important it is. Investing £100 pm, increasing at 3% p.a., into an ISA at a growth rate of 9% p.a. would, after thirty years, produce an ISA fund of £227,239. Investing £100 pm (before tax relief), increasing at 3% p.a., into a personal pension at a growth rate of 9%pa would, after thirty years, produce a pension fund of £284,048. That's £56,809 or 25% more money for nothing. Furthermore, it's outside of your estate for Inheritance Tax and protected from creditors.

When you take the benefits, 25% will be paid free of income tax and the remaining fund will be paid net of income tax. So pensions are effectively tax-deferred savings vehicles.

If you don't have a pension, or you want to use the pension I use with my clients at Lexington Wealth, then go to Lexo.co.uk and open an account today.

How much to save

The million-pound question is, 'How much do I need for retirement?' In 2006, Lee Eisenberg wrote a great book *The Number: What Do You Need for the Rest of Your Life and What Will It Cost?* In the book, Lee writes about conversations he has had with his friends and his wife about how much is enough. How much money do you really need to live the life you want, for the rest of your life?

I like this concept as I believe we all think we need more money than we do to be financially independent. I have seen far too many clients come into my office, working long hours, sacrificing family time and their health, just to keep chasing money.

How much you will need will all depend on the answer to two questions: what you plan on doing in retirement and how long you intend to live. This may sound facetious, but it's true. What do you intend on doing in your retirement years? Do you plan on cruising and seeing the world, or are you content with the local village fetes and your neighbouring family? It's not for me or anyone else to decide for you what you want to do during your retirement years, but I will say that many people retire with too few financial resources.

Money gives you choices. If you don't have big aspirations for yourself, it gives you choices to support, care and give to others - family, charities or your faith.

How long do you intend to live? This is a serious point to consider. At Lexington Wealth, my financial planning firm, for the last twenty years we have assumed our clients will live to age 100. Now I am starting to work with younger generations of clients, it's my belief age 100 may not be enough. If we knew when our life would end, it would be a whole lot easier to plan the party.

For most, if you save £100,000 for every £3,500 pa of income (indexing at 2.5% p.a.) you require in your, assumed 40-year, retirement, this is a good rule of thumb. The reality is that you will spend more in your earlier years of retirement than the later ones (potential care fees excluded), therefore the above rule of thumb is a guide. A financial plan is what you need.

For example, if you plan for an income of £14,000 pa in retirement, this would be four times the £3,500 produced from £100,000, so £400,000 would be required.

When you consider if you retire at 60 you may need 40 years of income at £14,000, this would be more than £1 million of income paid out. This is due to the compounding effects of inflation – it's not simply £560,000!

Therefore, retiring later helps with retirement planning income needs and if you have started later you may not have any choice but to retire later.

Deferring your retirement until age 70, assuming a 30-year retirement, you would need to save £100,000 for every £4,500 pa of income you require. Therefore, to retire with a pension of £14,000 you will need a fund of £312,000 – almost £250,000 less!

I have put a calculator on my website WarrenShute.com/ TheMoneyPlan/Calculator to help you – but remember these are guides not absolutes. We have made assumptions such as a 5% p.a. net investment return and 2.5% p.a. inflation. Drawing excessively on your capital in the early years will negatively affect the compound growth available for later years.

For a comprehensive financial plan either go and meet with a good CFP (Certified Financial Planner – you can find one here financialplanning.org.uk/wayfinder) – or contact me via my website warrenshute.com.

Workplace pensions

If you are an employee, it is very likely you have been enrolled into your employer's workplace pension scheme. These started on 1 January 2012 with the largest employers, smaller or newer employers rolling out over a few years into 2017. If you meet the criteria, you will be automatically enrolled, and payments will be made into the pension scheme by you and your employer.

If you are not a member, join now. Literally now. Stop reading, email your HR or the person responsible for workplace pensions and join. If your affairs are complex, seek advice.

There are three categories of 'worker':

Eligible Jobholders are aged twenty-two to state pension age (SPA – sixty-five to sixty-eight), earning over £10,000 p.a. or the payroll equivalent, i.e. £833.33 pm. If this is you, you are entitled to be enrolled automatically into the workplace pension and have your employer also pay into the pension on your behalf.

Non-eligible Jobholder. There are two subcategories of Non-eligible Jobholders: (1) people aged sixteen to twenty-one or SPA to seventy-five who earn over £10,000, or (2) people aged between sixteen and seventy-four who earn between £5,876 and £10,000 p.a. If you are in this category, you are not automatically enrolled, but if you ask, you will be enrolled, and your employer must also pay into the pension on your behalf. Great news.

Entitled Jobholder. An Entitled Jobholder is not really entitled to anything! They are sixteen to seventy-four and earn below £5,876. Entitled jobholders can join a workplace pension, but their employer is not legally obliged to contribute anything.

As you can see, it's a complex area. Short answer – join the scheme (unless you have complex pension needs requiring protection).

In addition to there being different categories of members, there are different contribution minimums. Your employer can confirm which of these will apply to you.

Contribution Amounts. The Contribution Amounts will depend on what definition your employer has decided to use as your 'pensionable income'. There are four options for them to choose from.

The finer detail is out of the scope of this book, but more information can be found at the Pensions Regulator's website*.

In summary, join the pension, especially if your employer will also contribute.

LISAs – Lifetime Individual Savings Accounts

These were launched in April 2017, and they allow anyone in the UK aged eighteen to forty to start a savings plan. The maximum allowance into a LISA is £4,000 p.a., and HMRC will credit £1,000 or 25% of your contribution to the account with tax relief. So if you invest the full allowance of £4,000, you will have £5,000 saved.

LISAs can be used for a home purchase or retirement and offer an excellent alternative for basic rate tax payers.

I have produced a guide comparing LISAs with the Help to Buy ISA (the predecessor). To download this guide, go to WarrenShute.com/TheMoneyPlan/LISA.

Pension consolidation

If you have worked for various employers, or started and stopped various pension savings over the years, you may feel a little unorganised. This can be said for thousands of

*(pensionsadvisoryservice.org.uk/about-pensions/pensions-basics/automatic-enrolment/how-much-do-i-and-my-employer-have-to-pay.)

individuals around the UK. They have had good intentions and started saving for retirement via a pension, and for one reason or another, they've needed to stop the payments. Rather than going back to the original pension and re-establishing contributions, or moving the fund into the new and hopefully improved arrangement, they start a new scheme. Multiply this numerous times over the years and you could have financial chaos.

If this is you, I recommend you pay a Certified Financial Planner a fee to research it for you. You can find one at the Chartered Institute for Securities and Investments' website financialplanning.org.uk/wayfinder.

If you would prefer not to, or are unable to find a CFP then visit my site Lexo.co.uk. This is a site which enables any client (with a minimum of £20,000 of investable assets) to access the same portfolios and wrappers as my clients at Lexington Wealth. Lexo.co.uk can do this at a fraction of the fee a traditional financial planner charges, because the majority of the relationship is automated. Financial planning should not just be for the wealthy; my vision is for it to be for everybody.

So, if you have £500,000 and you want to have a face to face relationship, either contact me at lexingtonwealth. co.uk or go to financialplanning.org.uk/wayfinder and find a Certified Financial Planner near you. If you have less than

£500,000 or you prefer to work online, go to Lexo.co.uk and start the process to investigate whether consolidating your pensions is the right decision for you.

There are numerous benefits in consolidating personal pensions. Some of these are:

- Ease of future planning of your retirement needs
- Ease of administration for your executors on your death
- Ease of asset allocation of the portfolio
- Potentially better or newer pension features and legislation when moving from older style pensions

However, a pension is not like your utilities. There can be drawbacks which prevent consolidation (pension switch). These include:

- Your existing pension has a higher tax free cash value which would be lost on a transfer/switch
- Your existing pension has a guaranteed annuity rate or a guaranteed fund value at retirement, which would be lost if switched
- Your existing pension has unreasonable transfer penalties, which make it not worth switching
- The new pension is less competitive than your current arrangements i.e. it's more expensive

This is why Lexo will not allow you to switch without an advised process. Lexo.co.uk charges a small fee to do an independent switch review for you.

Defined benefit transfer

A defined benefit pension scheme is a final salary pension offered by your employer. The pension offers you a guaranteed income at retirement, based on the years of service and your salary (however this is defined).

It is often the best advice to keep a defined benefit pension where it is, mainly due to the guaranteed features, indexation and spouse's benefits. However, when the pensions reform legislation came into effect, you were no longer forced to purchase an annuity at retirement. This coincidently combined with higher transfer values known as cash equivalent transfer values (CETV) from defined benefit schemes, due to lower gilt yields/interest rates.

Some members of defined benefit pension schemes have considered moving the fund away from the guarantee of the defined benefit to a personal pension. There are numerous pros and cons which are not for this book, but I would recommend you seek good quality independent financial advice at lexingtonwealth.co.uk or from a Certified Financial Planner at financialplanning.org.uk/wayfinder if you are considering this.

Summary

- The best time to save was ten years ago; the second best time is now

- Choose the highest investment risk which will still allow you to sleep soundly at night

- Automate your investment payment each and every month

- Choose your employer's workplace pension, or open a new pension

- Make sure you have joined and benefit fully from any employer's payment

CONCLUSION
Believing In Yourself

Very early on in my career, I understood that creating wealth – being successful with money no matter how much you had – was as much about psychology as skill set and process. It all starts and ends in the brain. Your beliefs around money will make you or break you.

> **Whether you think you can, or you think you can't – you're right.**
> **Henry Ford**

Right now, I want you to think what you would need to believe in order to be a money master. How would you be sitting right now if you were a money master? What would you be thinking? What decisions would you make? What would you need to tell yourself to be financially in control and on the path to ultimate financial freedom? How does that feel?

It's what goes on in your mind twenty-four hours a day, seven days a week that will ultimately drive your financial success. I can tell you to do this or that – pay this debt first, invest in this portfolio next – but if you have a limiting belief that says you can't or don't deserve to be a money master then the house of cards will come falling down. Look at the number of celebrity bankruptcies there are. It's not about how much money you have or can generate; it's what you believe that counts.

I want you to set yourself up for success. When you follow the actions detailed in this book your life will change, and we need to ensure you keep up with the changes. Take ten to twenty minutes each day, whenever is right for you, and just be.

In the 21st century, our brains never get a break. I love technology – I love what it has done for us as a society and what it will do in the future. Technology excites me, but I recognise our brains have become too busy, and many of us forget to stop. So, this final chapter of the book is all about making sure you are preparing yourself for the changes that will happen.

Mindfulness has hit the headlines in recent years with many celebrities practising it; meditation has been around us for centuries, starting in the Far East. Professional athletes understand the need to engage the brain. I want you to do this too.

You can use a guided programme, perhaps something available on the net. I have used the Headspace programme previously as I enjoy hearing Andy Puddicombe's voice. It's very soothing and works well. Or you can select some relaxation music to play, or you can sit in silence. I like to change things around for variety.

I have recorded a guided mind exercise for you to download to help you specifically to achieve and succeed with the 5 Steps of The Money Plan. Go to WarrenShute.com/ TheMoneyPlan/BrainTraining and download it now.

I want you to start by finding a quiet, comfortable place to sit. Ensure you won't be disturbed. With your eyes open, take a deep breath in, and as you exhale, relax. Continue breathing like this for a few breaths, and when you feel comfortable close your eyes. Continue breathing in and out in a relaxed way.

Now clear your mind. Depending on how busy you are in your head, this may take some practising, but what I mean by clear your mind is have no thoughts. If a thought enters your mind (a memory or something you need to do, for example), gently acknowledge it, say thank you and let it go. Don't fight it.

Focus on your breath coming in through your nose, filling your lungs, and release it out through your mouth.

After a few minutes of doing this, when your mind is clear, I want you to bring up an image of yourself celebrating financial mastery. Make this image bigger and more colourful, and then change the image to a movie; watch yourself in the movie enjoying the experience. Feel what it would be like when you have achieved complete financial mastery. Say to yourself what you'd say and see yourself enjoying financial mastery in full HD movie colour with those people who are important to you.

Keep this going for a few minutes before allowing it to fade away. Then clear your mind again, keeping the positive feelings of excitement and pride with you. Take a deep breath and open your eyes, feeling relaxed and refreshed.

Repeat this exercise as often as possible, but at least several times a week. Training your brain is like training your muscles – you can't go to the gym once and say you're fit.

You can continue mindfulness throughout the day by being consciously aware of what you are doing. When you are typing on the keyboard, rather than drifting away mentally, focus on your fingers touching the keys. Be aware of the sounds in the room and your feet on the floor. Be in the present moment. Every hour or so, make sure you take a moment to have a glass of water, look outside a window and really notice what's there. Don't just gaze, really look. Notice the different colours and the work of art that is nature. It is beautiful.

You can do this wherever you are now. Notice what's in front of you. Be present and less caught up in thought. Use your brain for thinking, not remembering.

If you liked this, I have put a special audio on WarrenShute. com/TheMoneyPlan/BrainTraining

I believe we attract what we are consciously aware of. Make a conscious decision to attract happiness and joy into your life.

Final thoughts
So, we have completed the Five Stages of The Money Plan and we now have the information and tools available to us to change.

Make a difference in how you feel and act with money.

Financial mastery is a lifestyle. Share your knowledge from this book and how you've developed yourself. You are now a student, but you can also become a teacher. Pay it forward. People who have a plan, a mission or vision in life are the most exciting to talk to.

Be kind to yourself. You may fall on your journey, so pick yourself up, dust yourself down and learn from your mistakes. Have fun, make your life bright and believe in yourself and your future.

> **We make a living from what we make, and a life from what we give.**
> Winston Churchill

As you may have noticed throughout the book, I am a big believer in health and wellbeing. I enjoy exercise and eating foods which support me. I am fascinated by diets and why some people succeed and others don't.

I was introduced by Bill Phillips to a study in the *The New England Journal of Medicine (February 2009)* which concluded that most diets are about the same, whether you are a no-carb eater, calorie counter or balanced nutrition planner. What the researchers did notice, though, was that people who dieted with a support group had a 225% improvement in their results. I found this fascinating. It's not about what you eat necessarily; it's about the company you keep.

Very early on in my career in the mid-1990s, I had a business with a wonderful team of people. We set up investment clubs throughout the UK and mainland Europe, the purpose being to share information and get people to invest as a team rather than on their own.

Fast forward to today. We have social connectivity online, so reach out to me and connect on Facebook at www. Facebook.com/WarrenShuteCFP. I'd love to hear your stories, successes and learning experiences.

We can achieve more together than we can on our own. Maybe one day it will be you visiting my office, like Mr and Mrs Peters, discussing your experiences, your highs and challenges.

As the great Zig Ziglar used to say, 'I'll see you at the top!'

Enjoy the journey.

APPENDIX

Lump Sum or Income Life Assurance
Typically, pound for pound, life assurance as an income is less expensive than a lump sum, so you may prefer to repay capital debts with a lump sum and provide an income to replace lost earnings.

Waiver of Premium
An insurance which can be added to the premium to ensure that in the event of an accident or sickness resulting in the inability to work, the premium is paid. This would not be the case in the event of a redundancy claim.

Terminal Illness
This is often an included extra to most life assurance plans, which means that in the event of the life assured being diagnosed with a terminal illness (fatality within twelve months), the policy benefits will become payable immediately.

Critical Illness or Serious Illness
This can be either a stand-alone policy, e.g. a Term Critical Illness plan, or a bolt-on extra to a life assurance term policy.

Indexing, Level or Decreasing Benefits

The benefits, either lump sum or income, can be arranged on an indexing, i.e. increasing, typically with RPI, or level basis. Lump sum benefits can also be arranged on a reducing basis. Typically, it would be wise to arrange benefits on an indexing basis. However, if you find after a few years your wealth is increasing through investing and repaying debts, the amount of life assurance required will be less. The indexation can be switched off with most policies – check the details.

ACKNOWLEDGEMENTS

I'd like to thank my clients of Lexington Wealth Management who have made me the financial planner I have become. Many of you have entrusted me and my firm with your family wealth for many years, we have grown together and I appreciate your business.

Paul Etheridge, for the hours of counsel and coaching you have provided to me, I will remember our Advanced Planners Group and the fun we had for as long as I live.
Carl Reader and Michael Tipper, for generously sharing your knowledge with me, thank you; you are both an inspiration.

My wife Nicky, children Oliver and Isabella, for being patient with me and allowing me the additional time our schedule didn't always allow to write this book.

My parents for always showing me love, which gave me the confidence to learn without the fear of failure.

THE AUTHOR

 Warren Shute is a chartered wealth manager and director at Lexington Wealth and Lexo.co.uk. Lexington Wealth provides financial planning and investment services to a select number of high net worth individuals, and Lexo.co.uk is an online platform offering access to a range of investment portfolios using the Dimensional Fund Advisors range of funds.

Warren obtained his Master's degree in Financial Planning and Business from Manchester Metropolitan University Business School in 2011, has held the certified financial planner licence since 2005, and has a Fellowship of the Chartered Institute for Securities and Investment (CISI) and the Personal Finance Society.

He was awarded the CISI CFP Financial Professional of the Year in 2017 and his firm was nominated as a Top 100 financial planning firm in the UK in 2016 and again in 2017 by CityWire.

Warren frequently contributes to broadcast and national media on financial planning and investment matters and regularly writes for The *i* newspaper. He is fascinated by the psychology of money and holds a master practitioner of neuro-linguistic programming awarded by Dr Richard Bandler.

He is happily married to Nicky and has two children, Oliver and Isabella. They live near the Cotswolds, England.

You can connect with Warren on:
WarrenShute.com

Facebook: facebook.com/warrenshuteCFP

Twitter: @warrenshute

LinkedIn: linkedin.com/in/warrenshute

Instagram: instagram.com/warrenshute

YouTube: youtube.com/c/warrenshute